EDITORIAL

All hail those who speak out

The brave stand up when others are afraid to do so. Let's remember how hard that is to do, says **Rachael Jolley**

49(03): 1/3 | DOI: 10.1177/0306422020958267

RUTH BADER GINSBURG is a dissenting voice. Throughout her career she has not been afraid to push back against the power of the crowd when very few were ready for her to do so.

The US Supreme Court justice may be a popular icon right now, but when she set her course to be a lawyer she was in a definite minority.

For many years she was the only woman on the court bench, and she was prepared to be a solitary voice when she felt it was vital to do so, and others strongly disagreed.

The dissenting voice and its place in US law is a fascinating subject. A justice on the court who disagrees with the majority verdict publishes a view about why the decision is incorrect. Sometimes, over decades, it becomes clear that the individual who didn't go with the crowd was right.

The dissenting voice, it seems, can be wise beyond the established norms. By setting out a dissenting opinion, it gives posterity the chance to reassess, and perhaps to use those arguments to redraft the law in later times.

Bader Ginsburg was the dissenting voice in the case of Ledbetter v Goodyear – in which Lily Ledbetter brought a case on pay discrimination but the court ruled against her – and in Shelby County v Holder on voting discrimination, an issue likely to be hotly debated again in this year's US presidential election. Bader Ginsburg's opinions may not have been in the majority when those cases were heard but the passage of time, and of some legislation, proved her right.

The dissenting voice in law is a model for why freedom of expression is so vital in life. You may feel alone in your fight for the right to change something (or in your position on why something is wrong), but you must have the right to express that opinion. And others must be willing to accept that minority views should be heard – even if they disagree with them.

Fight for the principle, and when the time comes that you, your friends or your neighbours need it, it will be there for you.

Right now, writers, artists and activists are standing up for that principle, not necessarily for themselves but because they feel it is right.

Sometimes they also bravely dissent when most people are afraid to speak up for change, or to disagree with those who shout the loudest.

Being different and on the outside is a lonely place to be, but the pressure is even greater when you know opposing an idea, or law, could mean losing your home or your job, or even landing in prison.

As editor-in-chief at Index I have been privileged to work with extraordinary people who are willing to be dissenting voices when, all around them, society suggests they should →

EDITOR-IN-CHIEF
Rachael Jolley
DEPUTY EDITOR
Jemimah Steinfeld
SUB EDITORS
Tracey Bagshaw,
Adam Aiken

CONTRIBUTING EDITORS
Kaya Genç (Turkey),
Laura Silvia Battaglia
(Yemen and Iraq),
Stephen Woodman
(Mexico)

EDITORIAL ASSISTANT
Orna Herr
ART DIRECTOR
Matthew Hasteley
COVER
Ben Jennings

ASSOCIATE EDITOR
Mark Frary
MAGAZINE PRINTED BY
Page Bros.,
Norwich UK

INDEX ON CENSORSHIP
indexoncensorship.org | +44 (0) 20 3848 9820 | 1 Rivington Place, London EC2A 3BA, United Kingdom

Supported by
ARTS COUNCIL
ENGLAND

ABOVE: Standing alone, activist Ieshia Evans is charged by riot police during a protest against police brutality outside the Baton Rouge Police Department in Louisiana, USA, 9 July 2016

→ be quiet. They smuggle out words because they think words make a difference. They choose to publish journalism and challenging fiction because they want the world to know what is going on in their countries. They often take enormous risks to do this.

For them, freedom of expression is essential.

Murad Subay is a softly spoken Yemeni artist with a passion for pizza. He produced street art even as the bombs fell around him in Sana'a. Often called Yemen's Banksy, Subay – an Index award winner – worked under unbelievably horrible conditions to create art with a message.

In an interview with Index in 2017, Subay told us: "It's very harsh to see people every day looking for anything to eat from garbage, waiting along with children in rows to get water from the public containers in the streets, or the ever-increasing number of beggars in the streets. They are exhausted, as if it's not enough that they had to go through all of the ugliness brought upon them by the war."

Dissenting voices come from all directions and from all around the world.

From the incredibly strong Zaheena Rasheed, former editor of the Maldives Independent, who was forced to leave her country because of death threats, to regular correspondence from our contributing editor in Turkey, Kaya Genç, these are journalists who keep going against the odds. These are the dissenting voices who stand with Bader Ginsburg.

Over the years, the magazine has featured many writers who have stood up against the crowd. People such as Ahmet Altan, whose words were smuggled out of prison to us. He told us: "Tell readers that their existence gives thousands of people in prison like me the strength to go on."

In this issue, we explore those whose ideas and voices – and sometimes, horrifically, bodies – are deliberately disappeared to muffle their dissent, or even their very existence.

Many people associate the term "the disappeared" with Argentina during the dictatorships, where we know about some of the horrific tactics used by the junta. Opposition figures were killed; newborn babies were taken from their mothers and given to couples who supported the government, their mothers murdered and, in many cases, dumped at sea to get rid of the evidence. The grandmothers of those who were disappeared are still fighting to bring attention to those cases, to uncover what happened and to try to trace their grandchildren using DNA tests.

Index published some of those stories from Argentina at the time because Andrew Graham-Yooll, who was later to become the editor at Index, smuggled out some of the information to us and to The Daily Telegraph, risking his life to do so.

We explore what and who are being disappeared by authorities that don't want to acknowledge their existence.

Thousands of people who are escaping war and starvation try to flee across the Mediterranean Sea: hundreds disappear there. Their bodies may never be found.

It is convenient for the authorities on both sides of the sea that the numbers appear lower than they really are and the real stories don't get out.

In a special report for this issue, Alessio Perrone reveals the tactics being used to cover up the numbers and make it appear there are fewer journeys and deaths than in reality.

The International Organisation for Migration's Missing Migrants Project says that 20,000 people have died in the Mediterranean since records began in 2014, but many say this is an underestimation.

Certainly there are unmarked graves in Sicily where bodies have been recovered but no one knows their names (see page 30). The Italian government has, as we have previously reported, used deliberate tactics to make it harder to report on the situation and to stop the rescue boats finding refugees adrift near her boundaries.

Also in this issue, Stefano Pozzebon and Morena Joachín report on how Guatemala's national police archives – which house information on those people who were disappeared during the civil war – is currently closed, and not for Covid-19 reasons (see page 27).

Fifteen years after the archive was first opened to the public, a combination of political pressure and a desire to rewrite history in the troubled nation has closed it. This is a tragedy for families still using it in an attempt to trace what happened to their families.

In Azerbaijan (see page 8), another tactic is being used to silence people – this time using technology. Activists are having their profiles hacked on social media and then posts and messages are being written by the hackers and posted under their names.

Their real identities conveniently disappear under a welter of false information – a tactic used to undermine trust in journalists and activists who dare to challenge the government so that the public might stop believing what they write or say.

This is my 30th and final issue of the magazine after seven years as editor (although I will still be a contributing editor), and it is another gripping one.

Over the years, I am proud to have worked with the incredible, brave, talented and determined. We have published new writing by Ian Rankin, Ariel Dorfman, Xinran, Lucien Bourjeily, and Amartya Sen, among others. And it has been a privilege to work with the mindblowing, sharp, analytical journalism from the pens of our incredible contributing editors over the years, including Kaya Genç, Irene Caselli, Natasha Joseph, Laura Silvia Battaglia, Stephen Woodman, Duncan Tucker and Jan Fox, plus regular contributors Wana Udobang, Karoline Kan, Steven Borowiec, Alessio Perrone and Andrey Arkhangelsky.

These people do amazing work: their writing is ahead of the game and they bring together thought-provoking analysis and great human stories. Thank you to all of them, and to deputy editor Jemimah Steinfeld.

They have told me again and again why they value writing for Index on Censorship and the importance of its work.

And because we believe that supporting writers and journalists is also about them getting paid for their work, unlike some others we have always supported the principle of paying people for their journalism.

Over the years we have attempted to go above and beyond, providing a little extra training when we can, translating Index articles into other languages, inviting journalists we work with to events, and introducing them to book publishers.

But just like the first time I ventured into the archives of the magazine, I am still amazed by what gems we have inside. We have recently reached our biggest readership to date, with hundreds of thousands of articles being downloaded in full, showing an appetite for the kind of journalism and exclusive fiction we publish.

Thank you, readers, for being part of the journey, and please continue to support this small but important magazine as it continues to speak for freedom. ⊗

They smuggle out words because they think words make a difference

Rachael Jolley *is editor-in-chief of*
Index on Censorship

CONTENTS

VOLUME 49 NUMBER 03 – AUTUMN 2020

MAIN: A government supporter removes pro-Hong Kong independence posters from a public space in Hong Kong, 2019

SPECIAL
REPORT

≡ The disappeared: How people, books and
ideas are taken away

Government hits activists' online profiles

Azeri journalists and activists are finding their online accounts are being hacked and altered, reports **Arzu Geybulla**

49(03): 8/10 I DOI: 10.1177/0306422020958268

ON THE SAME day that activist Rustam Ismayilbayli was arrested for protesting outside the ministry of education in Baku, capital of Azerbaijan, he realised his Facebook profile had been hacked. That was on 1 June. Two days later, while he was locked up, his lawyer informed him his Telegram account had also been accessed and that someone was sharing posts and messages while posing as him on both Facebook and Telegram.

Ismayilbayli was released on 15 June. One of the first things he did was change all his passwords, including on his Gmail account. But a couple of weeks later, he received another email from Facebook, informing him that someone was trying to access his account and reset his password – someone who was not him.

Ismayilbayli suspects that it was local law enforcement who broke into his phone and got hold of his social media accounts, and who sent a request to Facebook with his ID information in an attempt to change the password.

Aysel Umudova, a freelance journalist and a reporter with Berlin-based Meydan TV, which covers Azerbaijan, said her account was also intercepted using the same tactic. ID information was sent to Facebook with a request to reset her password. Umudova had never requested that change.

Umudova's and Ismayilbayli's examples are not isolated cases of journalists and activists

targeted online in Azerbaijan. Theirs are just some of the most recent examples of how people's social media accounts are being targeted in a new trend that aims to harass and silence.

Azerbaijan's track record on human rights and freedom of speech has been declining for decades. Documented by international rights watchdogs over the years, these violations, arrests and silencing tactics have become a regular occurrence.

Authorities have jailed scores of activists over the years, reaching a peak in 2014 when some 30 high-profile rights defenders, journalists and political activists were sentenced to lengthy prison terms.

Arrests, followed by the cutting of support to local NGOs, tough legal amendments and, eventually, the blocking of all remaining independent media websites have left one thing – social media – as the last free space. Facebook is the most popular platform, alongside Instagram and YouTube. And on these you can find plenty of posts on campaigns carried out by exiled activists, general grievances and comments on daily economic, social and political problems in the country.

Mission "digital crackdown" was only a matter of time.

Journalist Fatima Movlamli says she has lost count of the number of times her Facebook account has been broken into. Movlamli was targeted for the first time in 2018 when she organised a solo protest in response to a presidential election that many believe was rigged.

"Holding nothing but a sign that read 'Dictator Aliyev', I was arrested and taken to the anti-trafficking department of the ministry of the interior. I was 17 years old at the time and, despite

People's social media accounts are being targeted in a new trend that aims to harass and silence

being under-age, I was arrested, tortured and later blackmailed," said Movlamli in an interview with Index. The online blackmailing campaign against Movlamli took place shortly after she was released. Pictures and videos of an intimate nature, including Photoshopped images, were circulated on social media.

The efforts by the authorities to maintain control have been stepped up, explains Movlamli, especially in the past year. Among other measures introduced during the pandemic, an SMS-based permission system was

→ introduced in April. Citizens are allowed out only for basic necessities or if they have permission slips from their employers. The limits on movement were later extended to journalists.

In June, journalists were required to register online in order to get permission to work in the capital. Movlamli was among those who objected to this and relied on Facebook as a platform to make her voice heard. That is when her account was targeted again. In July, she lost all access to her account. Similar to the experiences of Ismayilbayli and Umudova, her ID information was shared with Facebook to request a password reset.

Movlamli is certain the perpetrators are the ruling powers. "They have access to all of our personal data and they have turned these attacks into some kind of trend now," she said.

Unless social media platforms disclose IP addresses and the names of those who have requested password resets, it is hard to prove who really is behind these attacks. What is certain, however, is that the perpetrators have access to sophisticated technology that allows them to bypass additional security layers.

Meydan TV is all too familiar with digital attacks against its reporters, its website (which is currently blocked inside Azerbaijan) and its Facebook page. The most recent attack was reported on 18 June when a significant amount of Meydan TV's content was deleted from its Facebook and Instagram accounts. Its Azerbaijani language Facebook page lost all content going back to 2018 and its Instagram page lost two months' worth of content.

In May, Meydan TV's Russian language page had lost all its content. The same month, its website experienced DDoS attacks.

The intent behind such attacks is clear: to limit information flow, to keep citizens uninformed and reliant on government media, and to cause as much damage as possible to independent news platforms. The time then invested in recovering accounts, battling with social media platforms over copyright violations and community standards and retrieving deleted content is time that could instead have been invested in exposing corruption, telling stories and informing the audience.

They have access to all our personal data and have turned these attacks into some kind of trend now

These attacks have not stopped journalists and activists from doing their work. It just makes it very hard – and, in the case of Amina Rustamzade, a journalist who was targeted online in a series of Facebook and Instagram posts, the consequences can be shocking. On 17 June, Rustamzade attempted suicide. Although she has recovered, she has left the platforms to avoid further damage.

Each post was reported to Facebook and Instagram. However, the level of harassment did not apparently violate their community guidelines.

Index has raised the matter with Facebook. A spokesperson from the company said:

"We take our responsibility to protect the privacy and security of people on Facebook extremely seriously. Facebook does not work with any government, including in Azerbaijan, to target accounts for hacking."

Clearly, there has been harassment, but Facebook says it does not have the context of the posts. Neither does it seem to have anyone who listens to these calls for help.

Unless someone has a contact within the company, the chances of being heard amid the platform's automated response and detection system are slim.

As Movlamli told Index: "Facebook needs to understand that in countries like ours, Facebook is not just a social media platform where memes and cute pictures of kittens are shared and liked. It is also [the only] place where we can get our voices heard. It's a place of hope." ⊗

Arzu Geybulla is a freelance writer focusing on technology in authoritarian states

Presiding over bloodshed

As Ugandans prepare to head to the polls, the voice of political opposition is being disappeared from the public space. **Issa Sikiti da Silva** reports

49(03): 11/13 I DOI: 10.1177/0306422020958269

DARKNESS SETTLES ON the Ugandan capital Kampala. The streets start to look like a ghost town. Heavily-armed security forces begin barking orders at hawkers and shopkeepers to close and go home. The Covid-19 curfew is about to kick off. Brenda, a 40-year-old street vendor, scrambles to pick up her stuff. Customers waiting to be served are dismayed.

"Please, let's all go home peacefully because these Museveni thugs have no heart. If you argue with them, they can easily blow you into pieces with their heavy guns. We are tired of this regime and its brutality which has lasted for nearly four decades," said Brenda, as customers dispersed in all directions, fearing for their lives.

"Will we ever be free one day in this country? Now, it seems to be getting worse as the elections draw near," a shopkeeper said as he served the last customer before closing.

"Nobody argues with the security forces," a Uganda People's Defence Forces soldier said, as he and his colleagues went door to door, ordering people to stay inside. "We don't want any excuse whatsoever from anyone. The president's orders should not be defied."

The UPDF, the Local Defence Units – an untrained, unprofessional and deadly armed civilian force – and the police have been accused of using heavy-handed tactics, including murder, to enforce the Covid-19 lockdown regulations.

Scores of people have been shot dead, including an 80-year-old woman who demanded to see a search warrant, while others have been shot and left with lifelong wounds, including a food vendor who was burnt with cooking oil by security forces.

For the past four months, Ugandans appear to have been witnessing the death of freedoms – especially freedom of expression – as Yoweri Museveni, president since 1986, uses what many see as dirty tricks to win a sixth term in office at next year's elections.

Sylvia Namubiru Mukasa, chief executive of Legal Aid Service Providers Network (Laspnet), told Index: "Many Ugandans have died at the hands of security agencies. Other violations include [attacks on] the right to personal liberty through arbitrary arrest and incarceration of suspects beyond the 48-hour rule.

"[It's a] violation of the right to food, with many going hungry; the right to education; and economic rights and livelihoods, especially for teachers, among others."

Incidents of intimidation and repression seem to be on the increase in Uganda. Opposition politicians' posters are being torn down, and many suspect such actions are by Museveni's people.

Supporters of presidential candidate Bobi Wine (real name Robert Kyagulanyi) have been targeted by security forces when they get together to welcome him. All gatherings have been banned and there's a belief the police are using this as an excuse to scare away the popular candidate's supporters.

On July 20, Charles Mutyabule, one of Wine's supporters, was knocked over and killed by a vehicle. Wine, meanwhile, has asked the government to investigate all lockdown killings.

Anthony Masake, of human rights and civil liberties organisation Chapter Four →

Opposition politicians' posters are being torn down, and many suspect such actions are by Museveni's people

→ Uganda, told Index that the brutality and extrajudicial killings by security forces were having a huge impact on democracy as Uganda heads to the 2021 general election.

"In addition to the fact that lives have been senselessly lost, the attacks are having a chilling effect on the exercise of freedoms. The killings, although mostly happening in the context of enforcing Covid-19 presidential directives, have encouraged self-censorship in political partici-pation," he said.

"These are familiar tactics of regimes that seek to narrow space for dissent, which is crucial for any free and fair democratic process. I think that the objective is to continue unfairly tilting the ground against opposition groups. An election is a process. What is happening now is already suffocating any idea that there can be a fair election."

The incidents are generating tension and radicalising the youth, with some openly swear-ing that it will be Wine or nothing come 2021.

"Ugandans are in Egypt and suffering at the hands of Pharaoh, who is Museveni. So we're all waiting for Moses, who is Bobi Wine, to liberate us and restore freedom, peace and prosperity," 21-year-old Alfred told Index.

However, Alfred's dream might not come true in 2021, as Wine and his party might not prove visible enough to unseat Museveni. The Elec-toral Commission has said that 2021 election campaigning must move online and on to televi-sion and radio to curb the spread of Covid-19.

Laspnet's Mukasa has lashed out at the com-mission's ruling, saying remote campaigning will disadvantage opposition politicians, who won't be able to access many media platforms.

"As a matter of fact, 90% of the media houses are owned by government bureaucrats," she said. "This is therefore likely to undermine balanced reporting and coverage of opposition politicians. In the previous 2016 general election, Forum for Democratic Change presidential aspirant Kizza Besigye was allegedly denied access on several media platforms, especially on the Uganda Broadcasting Corporation, which is state-owned media.

"On other occasions, the Uganda Communications Commission has issued directives restricting private-owned media stations from hosting opposi-tion politicians such as Bobi Wine… Museveni has [also] enjoyed more media coverage on both TV and radio through his national addresses on Covid-19."

In addition, she said a sizeable number of the population, especially in rural areas, had no access to electricity and the internet so would struggle to access television, radio, social media and social networks.

"The public will therefore be denied the right to access information as well as par-ticipating in the electoral process. Other groups that are likely to be marginalised from online campaigns include people with disabilities, including the blind and deaf," she added.

Masake echoed Mukasa's sentiments, say-ing popular participation through universal suffrage was an inalienable right of the people. "This fundamental right hinges on the right of people to be informed and have the platform to engage with political candidates for a two-way conversation," he said.

"The right to freedom of information, expression and assembly – both online and offline – are central to that participation. Even in a pandemic, it is important that these rights be limited only to the extent that is necessary, proportionate and justifiable in a free and democratic society.

"I'm afraid that the proposed restrictions in the context of digital campaigns do not meet this standard."

He said if public health arguments justified strict digital campaigns, the elections should be postponed by six months. "The framework for doing so is provided under the 1995 constitu-tion of Uganda," he said.

An election is a process. What is happening now is already suffocating any idea that there can be a fair election

As freedoms continue to disappear and the country reaches a political point of no return amid the rapid spread of Covid-19, millions of Ugandans are struggling to put food on the table. This is forcing them out of the house in violation of lockdown rules. Women appear to be the hardest hit, with thousands occupying street corners and public places to sell anything they can. At the same time, sex workers are particularly busy.

Asked if they were afraid of cops, one of them, a teenager, told Index: "I don't care about Museveni and his killers because none of them feeds me and my family. I have two siblings and a sick mother to look after. Is police brutality a new thing in this country? Ugandans are used to it since 1986. We've never been free in this country – not now, not before corona."

Macklean Kyomya, executive director of the Alliance of Women Advocating for Change, said sex workers were being targeted with violence, blackmail and arrest by police. "Women doing sex work and their families were already starving because local government officials have denied them food aid.

"Now they are being brutalised and traumatised, and forced to choose between starving, isolated with no income or working while risking their own health and safety."

Kyomya said Covid-19 was not just a health issue but one that had deepened pre-existing inequalities, exposing women to the vulnerabilities of the social, political and economic systems in Uganda.

As tension persists, many Ugandans fear that another Museveni victory could lead to violence.

"Walking into the election in the present structure of digital campaigns, brutality by security forces and overt partisan law enforcement will certainly result in one of the most contested elections in Uganda. It may lead to a constitutional crisis and social unrest," Masake said, urging the government to declare a state of emergency.

But, so far, the ruling National Resistance Movement has rejected calls for a state of emergency. The avenues for Ugandans to fight for their freedoms are fast disappearing. ⊗

ABOVE: Members of local defense units patrol the streets to enforce curfew in Uganda's capital Kampala, April 2020

Issa Sikiti da Silva *is an award-winning journalist from the Democratic Republic of Congo. He has travelled extensively across Africa*

"Silence got us nowhere. We need to speak up"

Rushan Abbas writes about trying to discover what has happened to her sister, who has disappeared in the Chinese state of Xinjiang

49(03): 14/16 | DOI: 10.1177/0306422020958270

THE SITUATION OF the Uighurs, a Turkic Muslim people group, is dire.

The Uighur homeland is referred to by the Chinese government as Xinjiang Uighur Autonomous Region but we call it East Turkistan. Xinjiang means "new territory" and this name alone reveals the government's determination to colonise it, while denying its history and our claim to the land.

The crimes they are committing in the concentration camps are made more horrific by their presence in the modern age. Perhaps the genocide of my people is unimaginable to many who choose to believe the narrative of a country where censorship is among the most severe in the world. The Chinese regime's actions now include every single act listed in the 1948 Genocide Convention, which the whole world – including China – is obligated to prevent.

The Chinese authorities seek to deny or defend the concentration camps and the slavery that has caused misery and destruction, but they cannot deny the witnesses whose tales have begun to resemble the horrors of the Holocaust. Regarding the intent of the Chinese officials, Zumrat Dawut, a survivor of the camps, told the Washington Post: "They want the extinction of Uighurs."

Gulzire Awulqanqizi told Radio Free Asia about her time detained in the camps, saying: "When we feel sad and cry, they say, 'You cannot cry now – you can only cry when it is your allotted crying hour'. At the crying hour, they shout at us, 'Now you cry!'" The tears of the Uighur people at this time could drown the world, but even tears are censored.

As Uighurs in the diaspora slowly come forward, the testimonies of abuse increase. The hellish choice to remain silent, hoping for a miracle, unable to speak a word against this tormentor, is weighed against a second option: to exercise the human right to speak out, which can lead to further loss of human rights for family members.

The weight of this decision is placed upon Uighurs themselves rather than the guilty party: the Chinese communist regime. Many Uighurs have made the choice to remain silent in the hope of saving their family members, only to watch them disappear anyway, and so it becomes clear: silence will not save them. Perhaps rather than being silent we must shout. These horrors are here, and there is testimony about them, as the world resolutely trudges towards making the same mistakes of not speaking up or taking action. So here I am to scream.

The tears of the Uighur people at this time could drown the world, but even tears are censored

UNITED We Are ONE VOICE

WHERE IS OUR HUMAN RIGHTS?

China, STOP Harvesting

ONE VOICE, TAKE ONE STEP
TH US AGAINST CHINA'S
NCENTRATION CAMPS

As a Uighur-American, I have been an activist for years, but even with all my experience I was unprepared for the personal suffering inflicted on my entire family when the Chinese government abducted my sister, Gulshan Abbas, in Urumqi in September 2018. This was a retaliatory response to my public advocacy in the USA when my husband's entire family disappeared into the camps. Now this burden of guilt is borne not just by me but by my sister's daughters.

My nieces are here in the USA, raising their children without a grandmother. My sister is a retired doctor, a gentle and non-political person. Her silence did not keep her safe, and while it seems that my vocality condemned her, I – like all Uighurs – must remind myself of the truth that my actions did not cause this. The tyrannical actions of China's leaders did.

I have been a US citizen for more than a quarter of a century, yet the long arm of the Chinese communist regime has extended its reach across borders to ravage my heart by jailing the only people it could, and it is repeating these attacks regularly against Uighurs in every country to silence them.

How can human beings endure these injustices? When I speak up, I am the one who is abused in the media, who is accused of being a CIA operative and who faces other accusations that fail to address my message. China spends millions of dollars to run its propaganda, and even accuses me of stealing pictures to use as my missing relatives. The →

ABOVE: Rushan Abbas (centre) and others at a protest in the USA to raise awareness about the treatment of Uighurs

The absolute disgust that should be felt by all continues to be stifled by the many organisations infiltrated by or answering to the Chinese Communist Party

→ truth is that Chinese officials are frightened of me and must shoot the messenger, because they cannot answer the message.

Truth prevails, and truth is something that terrifies the Chinese state, which makes every effort to conceal the truth from its own people. The question of how these efforts are being supported by Western defenders of the Chinese regime is the one that should be asked more often. I will continue to raise it.

Some in the West have joined in China's narrative to claim that Uighurs' stories are propaganda by the West to distract from its own crimes and are used merely to wage war on China and socialism, yet many Uighurs who are speaking out are not in Western countries at all. Freedom of speech is more valuable than these misled individuals realise, and they choose to abuse it to defend countries without such freedoms.

The absolute disgust that should be felt by all continues to be stifled by the many organisations infiltrated by or answering to the Chinese Communist Party. Certain universities, places where ideas should be freely shared, are now bowing to Chinese pressure and censoring. Hollywood films are increasingly produced with Chinese money, and many "influencers" of the "woke" causes on social media remain silent. Fashion brands are benefiting from materials produced by Uighur forced labour.

Never again, the international community swore, yet here we are.

The free world must wake up. It cannot maintain freedom while continuing to seek the fleeting benefits of Chinese money. How valuable is human life? How much is my sister's life worth? How anyone can choose to defend

these most horrifying atrocities and infliction of human suffering is astounding, and history will judge harshly those who do so. China can be silenced by the truth, but we will not be silenced because of the truth.

It is long overdue for the international community to take action against this regime which not only censors the tears of the people within its borders but actively strives to censor and shape the narrative outside its borders as well. Many actions are needed to address the long reach of the Chinese regime, and protecting those who tell the truth is a large part of that.

It has been suggested that the USA should publish intelligence documents in co-operation with other foreign intelligence agencies, and this could be an important step, too.

While the world seems reluctant to confront reality, we must acknowledge that this threat will not stop with the calamity of the Uighurs. Today it is my people, tomorrow it will be someone else's. Supporting truth and adding your voice to those who speak out should not be a choice but a necessity in order for free speech to survive in our world.

We must act now, before it is too late. ⊗

Rushan Abbas is an Uighur-American activist and advocate from Xinjiang. She is the founder and executive director of the non-profit Campaign for Uyghurs

ABOVE: An Uighur woman at a bazaar in Hotan, Xinjiang, May 2019

"The idea is to kill journalism"

Kashmiri journalists talk to **Bilal Ahmad Pandow** about being taken hostage, threats and surveillance when they report on the news

49(03): 17/19 I DOI: 10.1177/0306422020958271

"**THE FEAR IS** so palpable that most newspapers have chosen to become the extension arm of the state rather than being a watchdog of society," journalist Gowhar Geelani told Index, talking about the new climate that Kashmiri journalists are forced to operate within. According to Geelani, the critique of government policies has disappeared from newspaper columns and the news sections.

Covering this region, Indian-administered Jammu and Kashmir, has always been challenging but six months on from new tougher regulations, many say things have never been this bad.

The Indian government imposed direct rule over the region in August 2019 after revoking nearly all of Article 370, a provision in the Indian constitution that provided some autonomy to the region. But pressure on media freedom was racheted up even further with the introduction of the New Media Policy 2020. Journalists were, of course, already operating under tremendous pressure – harassment,

intimidation, the choking of advertisement revenue, imprisonment, draconian laws and a communication blockade – all of which are forcing journalists to self-censor.

Many journalists had witnessed attacks and some have lost their lives, such as Shujaat Bukhari, editor of a local English daily, who was killed outside his office in 2018.

Qazi Shibli, editor of The Kashmiriyat, an online news portal based in Kashmir, was released on 25 April this year after spending nine months in a prison in Uttar Pradesh, more than 900 kilometres away from his home. Shibli was detained again by local police on 31 July and held for 17 days.

"It is very tough to get out in the field with such a sorry state of history of harassment and such strict restrictions. We have to go on telling ourselves this is our reality, we live this every day. This is unfortunately the new normal, we have to tell ourselves, we will risk, we will report the truth and then we might get shot," Shibli said.

Geelani, who has worked in the past for German news organisation Deutsche Welle, was recently charged under the Unlawful Activities (Prevention) Act. Geelani believes that the very idea of journalism has disappeared. He feels that journalists, opinion makers and civil society voices are deeply concerned not only about freedom of expression but also about freedom after expression.

"The constant surveillance of the written or spoken word from the state apparatus is Orwellian in nature. The idea is to kill independent journalism and criminalise opinions in Kashmir," he said.

Shahana Bashir Butt, a broadcast journalist working for Press TV, has been covering Kashmir for the past 12 years. She told Index that the little sense of security that the people of Kashmir used to have earlier is lost now.

"Earlier, reporters would report facts as they are or would do a little bit of editing as per the demand of the organisation, but now the entire process of information seems to be censored. It passes through many gates and by the time it reaches the audience the essence or meaning is lost," she said.

> *This is unfortunately the new normal, we have to tell ourselves, we will risk, we will report the truth and then we might get shot*

Restrictions have killed many stories in
Kashmir that would otherwise have made big
headlines, Butt believes.

Despite the digital threats that are associated with using VPNs, journalists here are
forced to use them. With the restricted speed
of the internet in Kashmir since August last
year and the frequent bans on social media,
VPNs are essential.

"I have to ask for extended deadlines,"
Shibli said. "The sort of scrutiny one is under,
it gets really tough. Unread messages in my
inboxes are often read, even before I read them
… this is the sort of scrutiny I am under."

Journalists work by adopting creative and
novel means at huge personal risk. Sharing his
and others' experiences, Geelani says that in the
absence of internet services and communication

The fear is so palpable that most newspapers have chosen to become the extension arm of the state rather than being a watchdog of society

channels, many journalists write stories on the ground, store them on thumb drives, book flights to Delhi or elsewhere to access the internet, and then send the emails to the respective organisations.

Not all journalists are tech-savvy, though, he says. "I was obviously helped by some of our younger colleagues who do understand the cyber world more than we do."

A few years ago, in order to get news out, many journalists would write stories and then ask friends working in television to make small videos of them, which could then be sent to newspaper offices via the outside-broadcast vans.

Geelani says that the New Media Policy is "dictatorial and straight from the Nazi manual". He says it grants unbridled powers to a clerk in the department of information and public relations to initiate criminal proceedings against editors, proprietors and journalists for what he or she deems to be "fake news", "unethical", "seditious" or "anti-national".

In a letter published in May, UN experts expressed serious concern over the working conditions of journalists in Kashmir who were booked under a different act, the Unlawful Activities Act. The letter stated that a "free, uncensored and unhindered press and other media constitute one of the cornerstones of a democratic society".

The muzzling and suppression of independent voices is resulting in a fabricated narrative of Kashmir as a peaceful area of India. "The state has sunk deep into the belief of 'my way or the highway', which is unfortunate in any democratic set-up," Shibli said.

Geelani describes himself as an optimistic person but said: "I see hopelessness and helplessness all around. I fear that darker days lie ahead." Many journalists, including senior and accomplished ones, have been summoned to police stations, interrogated over their routine stories for hours, and mentally harassed, with criminal cases registered against several of them. "What I fear is that journalism will be converted into stenography, where a journalist will be forced to be the mouthpiece of the powers-that-be. Such are the unbridled powers that the bureaucracy and police enjoy in Kashmir. Big Brother is always watching you – the Ministry of Truth and the Ministry of Love, as Orwell described in Nineteen Eighty-Four."

Based on her experience working in Kashmir, Butt predicts a bleak future for journalism here. "I know journalism will die a slow death and new journalism will be born that will be 'mouthpiece journalism' or a one-sided narrative," she said.

But despite all the challenges that the media face in the region, the value of fighting to get the truth out is not going away easily, according to Shibli. "The journalist fraternity in Kashmir has inherited the principles of truthfulness; hence cowing down to dissolve themselves into these false perceptions is defiance of an inherent tradition, which not many choose." ⊗

Bilal Ahmad Pandow *is a researcher and freelance journalist based in Srinagar, Jammu and Kashmir*

What has the government got to hide?

Ireland's new government is now considering a bill that would delete the records of institutional abuse survivors for at least 75 years. **Jessica Ní Mhainín** speaks to some of the victims

49(03): 20/21 I DOI: 10.1177/0306422020958272

"**WE KEEP SAYING** these are historical abuses. They're not. They continue into the present," Mary Harney told Index, referring to abuse perpetrated by the Catholic Church and the state for most of the 20th century in Ireland. Harney has many questions about what exactly happened to her as a child – and why. She endured years of abuse after being illegally fostered when she was two and being sent to The Good Shepherd Industrial School in Cork at the age of five. But rather than attempting to answer these questions, the Irish government is proposing to seal her records until at least 2095.

"We're all born with inalienable human rights, but ours were taken away and they haven't been restored," she said.

Ireland's new government must now decide whether to proceed with the controversial Retention of Records Bill or to scrap it, as Harney and many other survivors would have them do. The bill proposes to "seal" all survivor testimony which was submitted in the 2000s to state investigations into abuse in residential institutions, all administrative records, and evidence relating to all operations in general – for at least 75 years.

"Why Ireland is insisting on this craziness… I mean it's secrecy to the nth degree," said Harney.

The bill does not provide for survivors to be given a copy of their own testimonies or asked whether they wish their testimonies to form part of the national historical record during their lifetimes.

Harney was one of four survivors who spoke to a joint parliamentary committee about the bill last November.

Consideration of the bill was deferred, and Fiona O'Loughlin, who was chair of the committee at the time, told Index: "I was moved to tears by the testimonies of the survivors.

"All we could do was defer it. We didn't have the right to say 'This can't happen'."

She said that Joe McHugh, then the education minister, and his department put "a lot of pressure" on the committee to try to convince them not to meet the survivors at the pre-legislative stage.

"But it was something that, as chair of the committee, I insisted on," she said. "I think it was hugely, hugely important and it would have been completely wrong to go ahead and make a decision without having their input."

The bill lapsed with the dissolution of parliament in January, prior to elections in February.

The decision about whether to continue with the bill now lies in the hands of the new minister for education, Norma Foley, who was appointed in June 2020. "I have no doubt that this proposed bill should not go ahead," O'Loughlin told Foley in parliament on 28 July. But, as yet, Foley has given no indication of her intentions.

"What has the government got to hide?" Harney asked when she spoke to Index. "What is it? We don't know. We don't know why they're doing this."

Questions have been raised – not only by survivors but by academics, lawyers and archivists – about why the Irish government is seeking to adopt such draconian legislation. When introducing the bill in April 2019, McHugh claimed that it was needed in order to overturn current legislation which would see the destruction of the records.

But multiple legal experts contest this.

"The constitutional right to a 'good name' of those who might be seen as wrongdoers if records are released seems to be one rationale for

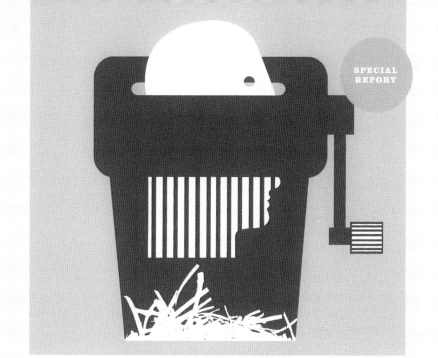

the secrecy," said Maeve O'Rourke, a lecturer at the Irish Centre for Human Rights, who has been working with and on behalf of survivors since 2009. "However, survivors' legal rights to their own data, and to speak freely and participate in truth-telling, are not being given adequate, or any, effect."

Harney, who is 71, and has been campaigning for the rights of survivors for more than 50 years, said: "I hate the word 'victim' or 'survivor', but that's what they are – that's what we are."

She says that being allowed to access her records would "go a long, long way" towards healing the trauma she suffers every day.

But what she fears most about the enactment of the bill is that she and other survivors will die without seeing their documents.

"Even if they extend it for 10 years, for some of us that'll be too late," she said. "I don't know if that's the intention, but it sure feels like it for us."

Harney, who has just finished writing her Master of Laws thesis, Denied Until They Die, is also concerned that the records will be withheld from academics and researchers.

"We are denying further generations the knowledge of what happened in their own country," she said.

O'Rourke shares this concern. "Denying survivors the opportunity to place their testimonies – if they wish, voluntarily – in a national archive creates a risk that future generations will not learn of this history," she said.

And Harney added: "The preponderance of protection is always on the side of the official

entities of Ireland, the official bodies – the official and religious bodies. It has never been with the victims of abuse."

She is also concerned about the safekeeping of the records while they are in the hands of the state. In the late 1980s and 1990s she was told that many records, including some of her own, had been destroyed in a fire.

"I tell you what, we're very lucky Ireland's still standing, because the amount of fires that Ireland seems to have had when people are inquiring for their identities... The whole of Ireland should have been wiped out."

When asked whether she believed her testimony to the parliamentary committee would make a difference, she said: "We know they heard us with respect, we know their intentions may be honourable – but intentions are not enough. We need action.

"All of them have stood up there and said 'This is all wrong, we have to put this right', and yet the one thing we want, the one thing that's ours by right, is our access to identity," she said, referring to the country's political leaders.

"It's as if we are being treated exactly the same as we were in the institutions: don't speak, listen, and do what you're told. We're in charge and we're going to give you this, and that's it." ⊗

Jessica Ní Mhainín is senior policy research and advocacy officer at Index

We keep saying these are historical abuses. They're not. They continue into the present

Don't show and tell

Many shows have been removed from TV channels and streaming services as they are no longer considered appropriate. **Orna Herr** investigates the new trend

49(03): 22/23 I DOI: 10.1177/0306422020958274

"**D**ON'T MENTION THE war! I mentioned it once but I think I got away with it," hissed Basil Fawlty in a line from Fawlty Towers that is still widely quoted more than 40 years later. The Germans – the episode in which Fawlty tries and fails to not mention the war – is the highest rated episode on IMDB of Fawlty Towers, which was named best British comedy of all time as recently as 2019. But a viewer visiting UKTV, the streaming service that hosts Fawlty Towers, on 11 June would have found that this episode was missing from the archive. It had been removed as it "contains racial slurs", UKTV said on its Twitter feed.

The episode features a hotel guest using racist language to refer to the West Indies cricket team. UKTV said it needed to be reviewed, and later reinstated it with a message at the start of the episode warning viewers that it contained "potentially offensive content and language".

This happened 17 days after the killing in the USA of George Floyd. The temporary removal of The Germans from UKTV was part of a trend on both sides of the Atlantic, with TV channels and streaming services removing episodes of programmes because they contained racist language or used blackface. More than a dozen shows streamed in the UK and the USA have had episodes prefixed with warnings or removed, or had entire series taken down, according to Index research, and at least four shows have been removed from Australian and New Zealand Netflix .

John Cleese, who played Fawlty in The Germans, was against the review of the episode, telling Australian news outlet The Age that some people "understand that if you put nonsense words into the mouth of someone you want to make fun of, you're not broadcasting their views, you're making fun of them". In contrast, creators of modern shows were instrumental in episodes of their programmes being removed from streaming services.

Is "disappearing" shows that contain language and content that is now more widely deemed as offensive an appropriate and effective response, or is it censorship and an attempt to rewrite history?

Kunle Olulode, director of Voice4Change, argued that left-wing politics had "traditionally rallied against" censorship, but in terms of racist content it is something "advocates of freedom of speech and freedom of expression now have to struggle with".

He told Index: "Whereas censorship in the past, in terms of Mary Whitehouse, has been about, I suppose, curtailing means of expression because of conservative values, today what's

THE DISAPPEARING ACTS

LITTLE BRITAIN
Removed from BBC iPlayer on 9 June
Sketch show that aired on the BBC between 2003 and 2007 starring Matt Lucas and David Walliams. Little Britain included characters of different ages, sexes, gender identifications, sexualities, disabilities and races, all played by Lucas and Walliams, both white men. The show in its entirety has been taken off streaming services.

A BBC spokesperson said: "There's a lot of historical programming available on BBC iPlayer, which we regularly review. Times have changed since Little Britain first aired so it is not currently available on BBC iPlayer."

SCRUBS
Removed from Hulu on 24 June
US hospital-based comedy-drama that aired on NBC and ABC between 2001 and 2010. It stars Zach Braff, Sarah Chalke and Donald Faison as part of an ensemble cast. Three episodes of the show

different is these things are advocated as radical and liberating gestures to protect people from harm." (Whitehouse was a British conservative activist who campaigned against what she considered to be offensive content on the BBC.)

Olulode said he believed there was a need for awareness of context and intention of racist content, highlighting HBO's decision in June to remove 1939 film Gone With the Wind from its archive before replacing it prefixed with videos discussing its historical context. He said today's critics had "a lack of understanding of satire", and underestimated the intelligence of the audience.

Referring to the use of blackface in 21st-century comedy, Olulode said: "I think they are comedies and they are send-ups of social life, and race is a component of that, and it seems to me what we're increasingly saying is that race is off limits in terms of humour.

"Part of it is certainly to do with more awareness and a growth, maybe, in terms of our political understanding, but there's another aspect to it which is actually a bit of a closing of the mind and … an inability to be able to

What we're increasingly saying is that race is off limits in terms of humour

appreciate the ability of people to distinguish from fantasy or fiction and real life."

Manick Govinda, a freelance arts consultant, echoed Olulode, telling Index that the public should be allowed to judge.

"Streaming or broadcasting companies should treat the public intelligently, [and understand] that we are able to discern the context and content of blackfacing," he said.

"Recent examples of blackfacing are ambiguous and no longer hold the racist messaging [that] programmes like The Black and White Minstrel Show did." ⊗

Orna Herr *is editorial assistant at Index*

---

were removed from the streaming service at the request of the creator of the show, Bill Lawrence. The episodes in question featured actors using blackface.

Lawrence said on Braff and Faison's podcast: "We didn't get asked to do this. I called [Disney] up and said, 'Hey, there's a bunch of episodes with blackface in it and I want to get rid of them'.

"The PC cancel culture on Twitter is like, 'Why did you pull the whole episodes? Why don't you just edit those moments out and put them back on?' And I said to one person, 'It's a pandemic. I don't really have an editing facility up right now'. I'll probably do that.

But the first thing I wanted to do was get them off TV because it bummed me out personally."

30 ROCK
Removed from Amazon Prime on 22 June
Satirical sitcom that aired between 2006 and 2013 on American channel NBC. It was created by Tina Fey, who requested that four episodes be removed from streaming services. These episodes featured actors using blackface.

Fey said: "As we strive to do the work and do better in regards to race in America, we believe that these episodes featuring actors in race-changing make-up are best taken out of circulation. I understand now

that 'intent' is not a free pass for white people to use these images. I apologise for pain they have caused. Going forward, no comedy-loving kid needs to stumble on these tropes and be stung by their ugliness. I thank NBCUniversal for honouring this request."

BO' SELECTA!
Removed from Channel 4 on 10 June
Sketch show that aired on the UK's Channel 4 between 2002 and 2009. It starred Leigh Francis and celebrity guests, with Francis playing the character Avid Merrion as well as impersonating celebrities, including black celebrities, by wearing

rubber masks. Francis released a video in which he apologised for the use of blackface.

He said: "I've been talking to some people and I didn't realise how offensive it was back then and I just want to apologise. I want to say sorry for any upset I caused whether I was Michael Jackson, Craig David or Trisha Goddard... all people who I am a big fan of. I guess we're all on a learning journey."

A statement from Channel 4 published by Digital Spy said: "We support Leigh in his decision to reflect on Bo' Selecta! in light of recent events and we've agreed with him to remove the show from the All4 archive."

Restaurants scrub off protest walls

Oliver Farry visits the Hong Kong businesses which have removed all signs of political messaging following the passage of the National Security Law

49(03): 24/26 I DOI: 10.1177/0306422020958275

ALREADY A SEASONED entrepreneur at 28, Terry Mok opened TeaBrush – a stylish cafe in a busy Hong Kong shopping mall – in 2018. Although the upheaval wrought by last year's protests has affected business, he has been unstinting in his support for them.

TeaBrush serves the sort of high-end flavoured ice teas that are as ubiquitous here as lattes and cappuccinos are in the West. One of its selling points is personalised messages on the drinks. Over the past year, many of the protest movement's slogans, such as "liberate Hong Kong, revolution of our times" and "five demands, not one less", have figured on the café's plastic goblets.

Since the passing of the National Security Law on 30 June, Mok has deemed those too risky to display, although there are still visible signs of support for the protests. These include action figures of frontliners in signature yellow hard hats and the familiar cutesy protest mascots, the LIHKG pigs.

The new law has forced many of Hong Kong's pro-democracy businesses – informally known as the "yellow economy" – to reassess what they can and cannot say.

Political stances by businesses in Hong Kong have historically been the preserve of pro-Beijing elements, according to Vera Yuen, lecturer in economics at the University of Hong Kong.

"Under British rule, businesses under the influence of communist China were doing this. There were department stores funded by Chinese government money, staff recruited from pro-CCP schools," she said. However, in recent decades, such positions have been rare.

Businesses are loath to nail their colours to the mast in either direction lest they alienate anyone. Some businesses perceived as supporting the government – known in Hong Kong parlance as "blue" – have incurred the wrath of hardcore protesters and had their premises trashed.

Risking a share of the mainland Chinese market is a great concern for many, but that has not stopped some businesses from supporting protesters.

Enterprises sympathetic to the cause have provided bottles of water and refreshments during marches, funded first-aid material, offered protesters meal vouchers and hired those in need of work.

But the National Security Law, with its draconian sentences for supposed secessionism, subversion and terrorism, has introduced a new danger. Antagonising consumers is one thing – risking lengthy prison sentences is another entirely.

On the night the law came into force, a number of cafes and restaurants scrubbed their Lennon Walls – collages of Post-it notes bearing pro-democracy messages – in case they fell foul of the new ordinance. Certain forms of dissent are now effectively criminalised, particularly if they are seen to advocate independence.

RIGHT: Pro-government activists remove a so-called Lennon Wall of posters from a street in Hong Kong, September 2019

Nam Fy, 32, opened a small restaurant serving Japanese rice bowls in Mong Kok last September, while the protests raged throughout the city. Many in his position would have kept their heads down but Nam was unabashed in his support for the protests, hanging pro-democracy posters in the restaurant and even broadcasting the protest anthem Glory to Hong Kong on a street-facing LED screen. It didn't do any harm to business, as pro-democracy diners flocked to eat there.

It's not a matter of what you can do but what you dare do

Direct ripostes from the authorities are less likely than an accumulation of lesser persecutions. Herbert Chow, owner of Chickeeduck, a chain of 13 children's clothing stores, had a lease renewal on one of them refused in

→ June after it featured a statue of the protest icon Lady Liberty.

Mok admits his own business has been shielded from trouble with the landlord by a sympathetic mall manager. But both he and Nam foresee increased health inspections and other pressures for dissenting restaurateurs.

Even before the National Security Law was brought in, Nam encountered police officiousness after a video of him remonstrating with riot police during a protest last year went viral.

Officers have stopped and searched him and issued fines for petty violations, such as using a kick scooter on the pavement, and Mok says he has been ordered to stop allowing other yellow economy businesses to use his offices.

Nam says he will still try to push the envelope, albeit in a low-key way, likening it to jaywalking. "It's not a matter of what you can do but what you dare do."

But, with friends who played an active role on the protest frontlines contemplating moving to Taiwan, he is aware there are limits.

Determining where those limits lie can be difficult, and businesses in various fields which have taken a pro-democracy position are grappling with a fog of doubtfulness.

Publishing is one sector in Hong Kong that has felt an increasing chill in recent years.

For decades, the city was the centre of Sinophone publishing, free from the censorship of communist China or Chiang Kai-shek's Taiwan.

But now, troublesome books in Chinese have a far greater chance of appearing in Taipei than in Hong Kong. As with signs in restaurants, titles are disappearing from bookstores.

Jimmy Pang, 64, has run Subculture Publishing for more than 30 years, bringing out books on topics of local interest and Hong Kong history. Though a vocal supporter of the protests, he says his books are far from the contentious material published by a group of Hong Kong booksellers who were abducted by Chinese security agents and taken to the mainland in 2015.

Even so, he worries about the current climate.

He says it is getting harder to publish "because publishers are reluctant to publish certain writers, and then distributors won't carry certain books".

The fact that many of Hong Kong's bookshop chains are owned by CCP-affiliated companies compounds this further.

It is the vagueness of the new law that bothers him the most. "Everyone in government is telling us something different about how it affects us," he said.

He also fears its arbitrary provisions, which allow police commissioners to issue their own search warrants, saying: "It's no longer rule of law but rule of man."

Two of Pang's recent titles – a global history of independence movements which barely mentions Hong Kong, and a book on China's 1989 democracy movement by veteran journalist Ida Chan – have drawn the attention of pro-Beijing social media and, as a safety precaution, he chose not to feature them at this year's Hong Kong Book Fair.

Such uncertainty in the face of a nebulous law leaves many in Hong Kong's yellow economy wondering where the red line lies – a situation that can only play into the hands of Beijing. ⊗

Antagonising consumers is one thing – risking lengthy prison sentences is another entirely

Oliver Farry *is a freelance journalist based in Hong Kong*

Closure means no closure

Political pressure has closed the library
housing vital information about Guatemala's
horrific civil war, report **Stefano Pozzebon** and
Morena Pérez Joachin

49(03): 27/29 I DOI: 10.1177/0306422020958276

THE DETAILS OF thousands of Guatemalans who "disappeared" in Central America's deadliest conflict can be found in the National Police Historic Archive (AHPN), but today no one can access it.

Fifteen years after it was first brought to light, the archive is being obscured again by a combination of political pressure and, critics say, a desire to rewrite history in the troubled nation.

Rafael Gonzales and Paulo Estrada, two relatives of the tens of thousands of *desaparecidos*, can no longer access the archive to search for their relatives' fate: not because of Covid-19 or social distancing but because the archive of the disappeared is itself being disappeared.

In the past two years, the governments of former president Jimmy Morales and current incumbent Alejandro Giammattei have restricted access to the AHPN, curtailed its funding and dismissed most of the staff. The archive, long treated as an independent institution with autonomous finances, has been placed under the control of the ministry of culture and is strictly regulated.

"What happened is that the archive opened up a discussion, and that caused fear," said Gonzales. Fear still runs through the spine of Guatemalan society 24 years after the peace agreements.

For years, the military establishment and the Guatemalan government had claimed that there were no archives from the civil war era. It had been impossible even to track down what happened to Gonzales's brother, Orlando, and Estrada's father, Otto, let alone find justice.

The discovery of the AHPN crushed those claims and shocked the nation.

Suddenly, millions of records and files compiled for decades were brought to light. There was finally proof that the police had been involved in the disappearance of tens of thousands of Guatemalans – from leftist activists to ordinary citizens.

"Everyone knew that the police did the dirty work for the military during the civil war, and there was the proof," Gonzales told Index.

Thanks to the United Nations Development Programme and foreign funding, the AHPN was run as an independent institution, employing up to 150 workers. Many were former leftist activists who had fought in the civil war and became archivists to find out what had happened to their brothers-in-arms.

Gonzales's own family was also political. In the late '70s, his sister was often at odds with →

RIGHT: Paulo Estrada in his early childhood with his father, Otto, and mother, Beatriz Velasquez. Otto Estrada disappeared in 1984

→ the military dictatorship which ran Guatemala during the civil war and she was threatened. Orlando, the brother, was not involved in politics but one night he was stopped at a checkpoint while he was travelling northwards towards the Atlantic to receive a shipment.

He disappeared, and to this day his family doesn't know what happened to him.

Their story is far from unique. Amnesty International estimates that up to 45,000 people were disappeared in Guatemala during the civil war — which went on from 1960 to 1996 – close to the astonishing rate of one out of every 200 of the population at that time.

As he was spending a lot of time in the AHPN, Rafael decided to film what he saw inside.

The documentary he produced with fellow filmmaker Anaïs Taracena is a deep dive among the kilometres of eerie shelves and dusted folders that compose the archive.

In the film, a woman comes looking for answers about her brother's fate and is brought to a daunting room where every wall is covered with mugshots of *desaparecidos*: men and women, young and old, gay people, priests – the whole range of Guatemalan society of those years.

The woman and the viewer drown into this well of pain, surrounded by the eyes of the victims looking into the void.

Her search is successful. In front of her

Gonzales thinks he will probably never find out what happened to his brother

brother's photo hanging on the wall she whispers to the camera: "This is what we, the relatives of the victims, have always known: that there are records, documents…"

For many Guatemalans, the AHPN represented a new beginning.

"It gave me much hope, because it's a source that one can consult when he wants," said Estrada, whose father went missing in the '80s, never to reappear.

"You need to understand, not all the relatives are in the same step of the process. There are people who only now are beginning to accept that maybe their folk are *desaparecidos*, so having a physical reference there to consult changed everything."

That reference puts the recent troubles of the AHPN under even further scrutiny. The removal of the archive from public eyes is only the latest episode of a series of attacks on historical memory that relatives of the civil war victims say started just as the conflict reached an end.

When the Commission for Historical Clarification published a report in 1997, blaming state security forces for 93% of war atrocities, little happened apart from a formal apology on behalf of the state for the actions committed during the war.

"Memory is just something that is not talked about, not on television, nor in schools," Taracena, the filmmaker who worked with Rafael on the archive documentary, told Index.

"The state wants to turn the page, be done with what happened in the war, and forget about it."

Taracena thinks the limits imposed on the archive represent a missed opportunity for the country to confront its past.

But this is not an issue limited to Guatemala. Many other countries in Latin America have experienced the trauma of having their own citizens disappeared by the state: Argentina, Brazil and Chile as a result of ruthless rightwing dictatorships; Colombia, because of brutal paramilitary warfare; and, most recently, Venezuela.

Fear still runs through the spine of Guatemalan society 24 years after the peace agreements

As in Guatemala, thousands of families in those countries will probably never know what has happened to their relatives, but truth commissions have been established in recent decades to preserve the historical memory.

In Europe, Spain had to wait three decades after the restoration of democracy to pass a Historical Memory Law and to have a debate about its past.

"In Guatemala we were moving faster: Spain took too long, 30 years. Here we were already having trials, investigations," said Taracena.

"The AHPN, the action of the Association of Forensic Anthropology in digging mass graves, those were a chance to have that debate [but] it was halted. The years from 2010 to 2016 were very good, lots of actions from NGOs in finding the truth, and all of a sudden it stopped."

Gonzales thinks he will probably never find out what happened to his brother.

Their mother, who spent the last years of her life fighting dementia while trying to preserve his memory, died at the beginning of this year.

"After she was diagnosed with Alzheimer's and started losing her memory, she took refuge in the memories of my brother and that was it until her death," he said.

One of her last acts before she died was to donate her DNA to the Association of Forensic Anthropology, with the hope it could one day identify her son. Gonzales did the same, and now he waits for another government to reopen the archives. ⊗

Stefano Pozzebon is a regular contributor to Index, covering Latin America, based in Venezuela. Morena Pérez Joachin is a photojournalist based in Guatemala

The unknown quantity

Thousands of people are disappearing off the radar in the Mediterranean Sea and are never seen again. **Alessio Perrone** investigates why

49(03): 30/32 I DOI: 10.1177/0306422020958277

ONE OF THE last boats to vanish in the Mediterranean Sea without a trace carried 91 migrants who had sailed from the Libyan coast and were hoping to reach Italy or Malta. Everything else, it seems, is shrouded in mystery.

The rubber boat was one of three to leave from Garabulli, Libya, overnight on 8-9 February. One of them was pushed back to the African coast by patrol boats. Another was rescued by Maltese authorities. The one with 91 migrants seemingly remained drifting at sea, calling for help that would not come.

"They were in complete panic and said the engine wasn't working, the boat was taking in water and there were people in the water," said Chiara Denaro.

A sociology researcher by trade, Denaro is also an activist with Alarm Phone, a group that provides a crisis hotline for migrants – to amplify their calls for help and document the silence and inaction of authorities.

Alarm Phone received a few calls from the migrants in the early hours of 9 February so, as usual, the activists alerted the authorities about the emergency and publicised it on social media. But nothing happened and, at around 5.30am, the group lost contact with the boat.

It was the beginning of a long silence. Because state authorities and militias in that area can save or push back a boat without the public knowing, Alarm Phone activists reached out to authorities in Libya, Italy and Malta as well as international organisations to try to find out what happened to the 91 migrants.

Some institutions showed no interest. Others mistakenly claimed the boat had been rescued, presenting flawed and conflicting evidence. Nobody knew. The group had disappeared, and what happened to them is still not clear. Denaro says that some bodies were found two weeks after the calls, but their identities were not established.

The story is all too familiar to the Alarm Phone activists. Migrants have been vanishing while attempting to reach Europe for years. The International Organisation for Migration's Missing Migrants Project says that 20,000 people have died in the Mediterranean since records began in 2014 – although many consider the number an under-estimation. Two-thirds, or more than 13,000, are lost at sea without a trace.

But the sea crossing is just one step in their journey: thousands are also unaccounted for after reaching Libya, or after being returned to the country where war and human rights violations make it difficult to understand their fate.

What most disappearances have in common is the silence in which they happen, said Denaro. She said some people disappeared because of

When they arrive in Europe, they are only numbers – nobody knows who they are: they are bare data, deprived of substance and bodies. They disappear without public opinion feeling the natural emotion of the act

the dangerous nature of their journeys, but there were also "political choices that make it happen".

It wasn't long ago that Italy was not only not criticised for its border policies in the Mediterranean – it was even praised by some human rights activists. In October 2013, after two boats sank near the coast of Sicily, claiming the lives of at least 600 people, the Italian government announced a military operation that employed navy vessels to patrol much of the Mediterranean up to 90 nautical miles off the Libyan coast. The operation, codenamed Mare Nostrum, is thought to have saved some 150,000 lives in a little more than a year.

But as the migration crisis heightened, the backlash mounted against the operation in Italy and the EU.

"It was terminated in October 2014 as a political choice," explained Arturo Salerni, the president of the Italian Coalition for Civil Rights and Freedoms (CILD) and a prominent human rights lawyer who, among others, represents the families of the victims of the shipwreck of 11 October 2013 in their quest for justice.

"From then on, European missions focused more on pushing them back than on rescuing them – and deaths rose," he said.

Italy and the EU focused on creating deterrents for migrants trying to cross. First, in 2017, a centre-left Italian government signed an agreement with Libya's Government of National Accord under which Italy provided funding, training and vessels to Libyan militias in exchange for tracking and retaining migrants – often in concentration camps where human rights abuses are well-documented.

Then, as NGO rescue boats attempted to make up for the lack of rescue operations run by Italy, Malta and the EU, Italy moved against them.

In 2018, then-interior minister Matteo Salvini closed Italian ports to NGO rescue boats. A year later, the country introduced steep fines for allowing rescued refugees to disembark.

According to critics, the policies turned the Mediterranean Sea into a place where the lack of third-sector organisations meant that human rights violations could be carried out with little risk, as Index has reported in the past.

"The little damage control that NGOs did could no longer happen," said Salerni. "This not only increased the number of shipwrecks but also made it impossible to assess how many boats disappeared and how many people drowned."

At least seven vessels carrying more than 400 people vanished without a trace in 2019 alone, according to IOM estimates.

Salerni thinks the disappearances have political value. "If the stories of the people who disappear, the families they leave behind, the severed relationships... if they came to light, it could push a part of the population – the most sensitive part – to demand that these things no longer happen, and these policies are discontinued," he said.

Seeing relatives disappear without any certainty of their deaths can wreak havoc in the communities of origin.

The husband of Oum El Kheir Wertatani, a Tunisian mother-of-three, left the country after the Arab Spring in March 2011. He called his brother the night he left to tell him about it but then was heard from no more.

Wertatani's husband was one of about 500 Tunisians who attempted to cross the

ABOVE: A vessel holding Libyan refugees floats in the Mediterranean Sea while a Spanish Search and Rescue plane patrols overhead in 2017

→

What most disappearances have in common is the silence in which they happen

→ Mediterranean Sea in March 2011 but disappeared. Some families say they saw their relatives disembark in Italy in TV footage, but their fate remains unknown, and authorities in Tunisia and Italy have been unable to provide any information about them.

Because authorities have provided no evidence of their relatives' deaths, the families refused to accept them and began searching and campaigning.

"The entire first year after my husband's disappearance was a nightmare," said Wertatani. "It was difficult to go and search. It was difficult to believe that what happened happened. And it's difficult to believe and understand that they reached Italy and they did not call."

The group has been pressuring institutions on both sides of the Mediterranean for nine years to obtain more information about their loved ones – largely to no avail.

The condition of the people who vanish at sea and their families, as in Wertatani's case, has drawn comparisons by some to that of the Desaparecidos, the young activists who were

forcibly disappeared under Argentina's dictatorship. According to recent research by Emilio Distretti, a senior teaching fellow of politics and international studies at SOAS University London, the term helps survivors, families and activists to make institutions accountable and call out the disappearances and border deaths as part of a concerted strategy.

Enrico Calamai, who served as the Italian vice-consul in Argentina between 1973 and 1977 and helped some young people to flee the dictatorship, is one of the most vocal advocates of the term New Desaparecidos.

"[The migrants] die in a media vacuum," he explained. "When they arrive in Europe, they are only numbers – nobody knows who they are: they are bare data, deprived of substance and bodies. They disappear without public opinion feeling the natural emotion of the act."

While he notes that there are differences from what happened in Argentina during his tenure, he says it is very similar.

"People disappeared, but those who weren't a parent or had links to the disappeared would not react, because they perceived them [as] 'other', like something different. There is the same indifference in Italian and European public opinion today."

The indifference seems to continue when the disappeared come under the spotlight and are made visible to public opinion. On 29 June, an aircraft operated by NGO Sea-Watch sighted a dead body trapped in the remnants of a half-sunk rubber dinghy.

"We do not know what happened there," Sea-Watch head of aviation Neeske Beckmann said in a video statement, "and especially what happened to the other people on the rubber boat."

The crew asked authorities to recover the body. Italian media picked up the case, and a petition started to pressure authorities to act.

Two weeks later, it was still there. ⊗

Alessio Perrone is a regular correspondent for Index, based in Milan

ABOVE: An unmarked grave in a Sicilian cemetery of a refugee who died at sea while trying to reach Italy. Many refugees who do not survive the journey are never identified

Tracing Turkey's disappeared

Archivists worry that this summer's law to regulate social media will make it harder to research disappearance cases in Turkey.
Kaya Genç reports

49(03): 33/35 I DOI: 10.1177/0306422020958278

THE RENAULT TOROS was the most popular family car in Turkey during the 1990s. Its dreamy, adventurous name came from the Taurus mountains, and the sedan model proved a hit among middle class and public servants. In 2000, the car was discontinued because of its carbon footprint.

For Turkey's Kurds, the Toros was injurious for a different reason. In the forced disappearance cases of thousands of Kurdish activists during the 1990s, the white vehicles played a key role. They became symbols of the disappearances because they were the last things activists saw before rogue state officials kidnapped or killed them.

This July, spectres of the cars and Turkey's army of the disappeared haunted the country again. The European Court of Human Rights (ECtHR) rejected an application by the family of Fahri İnan who, in 1994, was killed by a group of masked men who approached him in a Toros. Although the police identified the car's licence plate and its owner, he wasn't called in for an interview and, over the next 25 years, nobody was held accountable. In 2014, Turkey's Constitutional Court dismissed the case because it had passed the statute of limitations. With the ECtHR's rejection, the case appeared closed.

For the dead man's son, Serhat İnan, there was little closure, however, and he pledged to fight for the recognition of his father's death. I came across news of his struggle on Perpetrator Not-Unknown, a digital archive monitoring extrajudicial killings and enforced disappearances committed by state agents in the 1990s. Run by the Truth Justice Memory Centre, Perpetrator Not-Unknown comprises legal analysis and other articles on forced disappearance cases.

Emel Ataktürk, director of the Tackling Impunity programme at the Truth Justice Memory Centre, has spent her life working in Turkey's human rights movement. She views İnan's case as one piece in a large jigsaw puzzle.

"At the centre we focus on documenting disappearances," she told Index in the organisation's offices in central Istanbul. "Compared with a case lawyer, the information we amass is different. Instead of solving individual cases we try to see the big picture about forced disappearances."

The Truth Justice Memory Centre is a leading organisation operating in memory studies, a nascent field for Turkey's NGO world. Founded in 2011 and staffed by 20 human rights defenders, most of whom work full-time, the centre focuses "on enforced disappearances with an aim to reveal the elements and patterns of how this crime was committed and to bring the perpetrators to justice".

→   When the centre's founding team con-
verged in 2010, Turkey already had a slew of
respected human rights organisations. From
the Human Rights Association (IHD) to the
Human Rights Foundation of Turkey (TIHV),
these organisations proved their worth during
coups and under repressive governments.

"So, we asked ourselves, 'Why would
anyone need a centre for truth, memory and
justice'?" Ataktürk recalled. Founders agreed
that "a wall of denial" had defined the Turkish
republic since its foundation in 1923, and that
"the refusal to accept systematic human rights
violations had grown into a pattern of denial".
The centre would highlight this pattern through
extensive documentation.

At the time the centre was founded, the
human rights situation was different in Turkey.
Between 2008 and 2010, Turkey was imple-
menting the Copenhagen criteria, the rules
that define whether a country is eligible to join
the European Union. These include improving
democracy, the rule of law, human rights and
the existence of institutions that guarantee
minority rights.

"It was a positive period when viewed
from today's perspective. NGOs became more
visible and vocal," Ataktürk said. "When we
established the centre in 2011, the 1990s was
recent history."

The forced disappearances of that period
peaked in 1995 and then slowly decreased. It
was also the time when Recep Tayyip Erdogan's

political star began rising. As Istanbul's newly
elected mayor, he pledged to fight Turkey's "deep
state" and its rogue operations against the pious
and the Kurds. These promises, soon forgotten,
helped Erdogan become prime minister in 2003.
In 2011, he invited Berfo Ana, the mother of
Cemil Kırbayır, a victim of a forceful disappearance, to his office at the Dolmabahçe Palace.

Aged 103, this symbol of the forcefully
disappeared told Erdogan that she didn't lock
her door at night in the hope that her son might
return. "Don't lower me to my grave before
finding bones of my son," she said. Berfo Ana
died two years later, having not found her son.

For Ataktürk and her colleagues, winning the
trust of people such as Berfo Ana to document
their cases was key. "We met people who directly
suffered from forced disappearances, conducted
interviews with families of the disappeared, and
looked at judicial processes to see whether those
investigations progressed properly or were stuck
somewhere inside the system," she said.

This way they were able to display, in all its
concrete detail, systemic human rights violations in Turkey and analyse disappearances
using big data. As files about victims, culprits
and judicial processes piled on their desks, they
felt they had to "bring together separate cases
and analyse what they were telling us".

The centre staff did their best not to
re-traumatise relatives of the disappeared.
Psychiatrists and experts trained staff, asking
them to role-play. "One person would be the
relative of a disappeared person; in a short time
she'd believe she actually had a lost relative and
became muted and start crying." They learned
about the ethics of talking about the disappeared. Still, Ataktürk says many experienced a
second-hand trauma after these interviews.

Enis Köstepen leads the centre's fundrais-
ing work. "During its foundation, the centre
made a list of 1,353 forcefully disappeared
persons," he told Index. "This was the number
of disappeared whose bodies were never found.
Later some bodies were located, and the 1,353
number changed."

When I was a teenager in the 1990s I too
remembered reading horrific stories of forced
disappearances in newspapers.

What can we tell to those eyes that don't see, and to those ears that refuse to hear?

"When you live among events you know about them, but when someone asks you to prove they actually happened you notice you need concrete data," said Ataktürk.

So the centre set out to establish a database of the disappeared. It would comprise information gathered from human rights defenders and families, with the ultimate aim of creating social acceptance that "these disappearances really took place".

In this endeavour, the centre asked relatives of the disappeared to contribute their own documents. It also got in touch with lawyers who looked at these cases. "We said, 'If you trust us and allow us to work on documents you share with us, you'll contribute to a project that will also serve as a memorial for the disappeared'. It wasn't easy at the outset. But as documents began flooding in, a bigger picture began to emerge."

The centre made this data publicly accessible. It couldn't share all the data, so it filtered it and tried to show the phenomenon of forced disappearances in all its harrowing detail.

In this work it co-operated with the EU delegation to Turkey, Heinrich Böll Stiftung and OAK Foundation among others. Since 2011, the centre has published numerous reports including Enforced Disappearances and the Conduct of the Judiciary (2013); The Unspoken Truth: Enforced Disappearances (2013); and Holding Up the Photograph: Experiences of the Women Whose Husbands Were Forcibly Disappeared (2014). In a recent event organised by the centre, a relative of a forcefully disappeared activist asked: "What can we tell to those eyes that don't see, and to those ears that refuse to hear?"

The centre plans to bring together all the films, albums, books and exhibitions on the theme of memory.

But in 2016, an anonymous complaint about a culprit in one document almost led to the disappearance of the database itself. The police went through the social media posts of the centre's communication director, in whose name the database's domain was registered, and detained him. The database was no longer publicly accessible and, at the moment, the centre is making preparations to reopen it.

To Ataktürk, such developments didn't come as a surprise. A seasoned human rights defender and lawyer, she is not easily shocked by Turkey's tribulations. The new social media law passed in July upset her with its inclusion of "the right to be forgotten", which she fears will be used to conceal names of rogue state officials.

"The right to be forgotten will be a great problem in cases involving forced disappearances." she said. "It will have a negative impact on the struggle to fight impunity."

Ataktürk also represented Murat Çelikkan, the centre's director and founder, when he was imprisoned in 2017 for "showing solidarity" with a censored Kurdish newspaper.

Çelikkan was released after spending two months in prison, but bad news soon balanced good news. The ECtHR's latest decision on Fahri İnan, Ataktürk believes, was against "the spirit" of the European Covention of Human Rights. She fears that if the same refusal to process the cases is applied to others from the 1990s, this may negatively impact the struggle for justice on forced disappearances.

Still, the centre had some support. Engin Yıldırım, the vice-president of Turkey's Constitutional Court, wrote an opposition to the decision and quoted a report by the Truth Justice Memory Centre. "This cheered us a bit," Ataktürk said. "You know, this work resembles digging a well with a needle. At the moment all the doors are closed to us. But the political conjecture changes quickly in Turkey. And then anything could happen." ⊗

Kaya Genç is Index's contributing editor in Turkey, based in Istanbul

"There's nobody left to speak"

With lawyers and activists under huge pressure not to voice opposition, India's government is increasingly willing to trample on freedoms.
Somak Ghoshal reports

49(03): 36/38 I DOI: 10.1177/0306422020958279

AS THE COVID-19 pandemic wreaks havoc all over India, the democratic values of the country are being trampled by egregious violations of human rights, watched over by a largely silent media and public.

It is also a time when some of India's most outspoken activists are disappearing deeper into the prison system, with little sign of being released. The pandemic, which is forcing courts to function in the virtual realm, is giving an unintended fillip to the state to manipulate its institutions with impunity.

Around the middle of July, 80-year-old Telugu writer and activist Varavara Rao, who has been languishing in a prison in Mumbai without trial for nearly two years, was shifted to a hospital in the city after he complained of feeling unwell for several days. He was diagnosed with a slew of health issues and tested positive for Covid-19. Kept in the overcrowded jail, alongside at least 1,000 other prisoners who had contracted the disease, Rao had been susceptible to the virus. And so are the 11 others who, like him, are being held in Indian prisons under an often misused anti-terrorism law, the Unlawful Activities (Prevention) Act (UAPA).

The UAPA, according to Supreme Court advocate Karuna Nundy, not only reverses the burden of proof like many other anti-terror laws but also gives "untrammelled discretion"

RIGHT: A protester wears a mask of imprisoned activist Varavara Rao at a demonstration against the arrests of pro-democracy activists in India in 2018

to law-enforcement agencies. Cases filed under the UAPA, for instance, can be investigated by officers as junior as inspectors.

The current Indian People's Party (BJP) government keeps pushing back the boundaries around freedom and democracy and how it would like to operate. Laws such as the UAPA are no longer being invoked in conflict zones alone — they are becoming a common tool in BJP-ruled states to intimidate dissenters. As historian and political commentator Ramachandra Guha put it, these laws have become "naked instruments of oppression". He said: "Previously, when charges were slapped under such laws, there was a possibility of seeking habeas corpus. But currently, the courts seem to have become handmaidens to the repressive state."

Several commonalities bind the 12 detainees. They are all left-leaning politically —Rona Wilson fought for the liberty of political prisoners, Sudha Bharadwaj lobbied for the rights of tribal communities, and several others have spoken out against the government's agenda of creating a Hindu-majority state. Four of the arrested are well-known academics: Anand Teltumbde, a Dalit scholar and activist, is a professor at the Goa Institute of Management; Bharadwaj is visiting faculty at the National Law University in Delhi; Shoma Sen is a professor of English at Nagpur University; and Hany Babu – the most recent to be charged under the law – teaches English at Delhi University.

Most crucially, though, the 12 detainees are all linked to a public event called Elgar Parishad, held on 31 December 2017 in Pune, Maharashtra. They had gathered, along with a soaring crowd of thousands, to mark the bicentenary of a historic victory of the Marathas, supported by the lower-caste Mahars, against the British in the Battle of Bhima Koregaon (1818). At this meeting, the speakers condemned the surge of violence against Dalits and lower-caste people by the Hindu right-wing. This was the ember for a major conflagration,

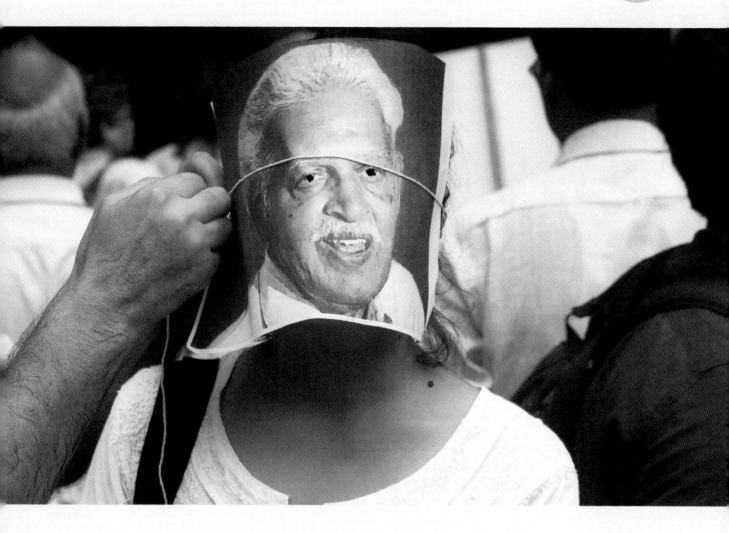

and a riot-like situation erupted the next day, fanned by long-standing grudges and existing tensions between the castes.

Later that year, this event became the flashpoint to arrest and detain Rao and the others. In subsequent months, more of their allies, who are accused of following a Maoist ideology (also mockingly called "urban naxals" by a section of the political classes), have been rounded up and arrested under the UAPA.

"These individuals have been jailed for their opinions," said Aakar Patel, a journalist and former head of Amnesty India. "[The] government has criminalised free speech as India has never seen before, including during the Emergency."

The right to dissent, though guaranteed by the constitution, has never had an easy airing in India. From the Emergency imposed by Prime Minister Indira Gandhi in 1975 to the brazen

Right now, the Indian republic is in the hands of people who never believed in its project as a secular republic

media censorship carried out under the watch of current Prime Minister Narendra Modi, an unbroken tradition of silencing thinkers, journalists and activists who refuse to toe the government's line is palpable.

Attempts are made to "disappear" them from the public eye and discourse. In extreme cases, such retributive measures may assume the form of outright violence, as was the case with the murder of journalist and activist Gauri Lankesh in 2017, by non-state agents.

I'm reminded of one line from Shakespeare's Henry VI: 'Let's kill all the lawyers'

→ In other instances, a law such as the UAPA, which can land a suspect in jail indefinitely with no hope of securing bail, takes care of the problem. It becomes a weapon in the hands of an authoritarian state.

India is no stranger to such draconian laws. In 1971, Gandhi's government passed the Maintenance of Internal Security Act, which gave law-enforcement agencies a wide brief to suppress dissidents. People were kept under preventive detention indefinitely, their homes were searched without warrants, and wiretapping was an approved mode of surveillance.

"While the Emergency may have seen the most widespread misuse of such laws, legislations like these have operated in Kashmir, in the north-eastern states, along the Maoist belt, in the states of central India, among other parts of the country for decades," said historian and political commentator Ramachandra Guha. "Subsequent governments, be they led by the BJP or the Congress, have been guilty of strengthening such misuse."

Social scientist and activist Nandini Sundar, who was similarly persecuted by the state on cooked-up charges, concurs with this view. In 2016, the Central Bureau of Investigation, acting on the orders of the Supreme Court, had filed a charge sheet against seven Special Police Officers and 26 leaders of a vigilante group called Salwa Judum, groomed by the Chhattisgarh government to combat the Maoist insurgency in the state. The original complaint had been made by Sundar and her co-activists, reacting against the violence unleashed on the poor tribal population by these militia groups.

Within days of their complaint, a report was filed against Sundar and her colleagues by the local police, alleging them of being involved in the murder of a tribal leader. The investigation dragged on for three years before Sundar and her co-activists were cleared of all charges in 2019 for lack of any direct evidence. In August,

the National Human Rights Commission awarded them compensation for the "mental harassment and human rights violations" caused by the false report.

"Right now, the Indian republic is in the hands of people who never believed in its project as a secular republic," Sundar said. "They are the ultimate 'anti-nationals' (a pejorative term for left liberals that has been given currency by the right-wing) and separatists since they want a Hindu *rashtra* [state], not this constitutional republic."

The tactics used to achieve these ends, Sundar added, include the "conscription of a loyal cheerleading media and subversion of all independent institutions". Most worrying among the latter, perhaps, is the subversion of the power of the courts.

Consider the conduct of the Supreme Court in the case of Gautam Navlakha, a civil liberties activist accused in the Bhima Koregaon case, currently held in prison under the UAPA. Last year, five judges of the apex court recused themselves from hearing his petition without citing any reason. "Recusal must come with an explanation of why and an acknowledgment, if any, of a conflict of interest," said Patel. "In these cases, it seems that the judges don't want to annoy the government."

Nundy added: "The fact that a law like the UAPA is being used to target lawyers themselves (Bharadwaj has represented the poor in many litigations) strikes a body blow to the rule of law. I'm reminded of one line from Shakespeare's Henry VI: 'Let's kill all the lawyers'.

"Lawyers are the bastions against violations of civil liberties. If you kill all the lawyers then there's nobody left to speak." ⊗

Somak Ghoshal *is a regular contributor to Index, based in Bengaluru, India*

Out of sight, but never out of mind

A new film explores the fate of just two of the many thousands of people who have disappeared in Syria. **Laura Silvia Battaglia** talks to those behind it

49(03): 39/41 I DOI: 10.1177/0306422020958280

"**I BELIEVE THAT THE** fact that the film talks about love – that of a young couple or between brother and sister – is a way to create connections. And it's a way to open a debate about forced disappearances in Syria."

Yasmin Fedda, the director of the documentary Ayouni ("Your Eyes"), has not let the coronavirus epidemic put her off, and after eight years of shooting she has released her latest work ("one of the most difficult ones in my life") online, come what may.

Following the online premiere, the film – produced in the UK by Elhum Shakerifar and Hakawati and supported by, among others, Amnesty International and the Doha Film Institute – is touring festivals in Europe and around the world.

"It's a very complicated time to release a film," said Fedda, "but we couldn't have done otherwise. Although being among the public is the best way to have some feedback, I keep receiving messages from many people who watch the film online and whose stories are very similar to the ones featured in the documentary."

The stories she refers to are those of more than 100,000 Syrian families who, after nine years of war, are looking for their disappeared relatives. The more

places where the documentary is screened, the more Fedda bumps into other families with similar stories.

Ayouni revolves around two main storylines, both of which share a common theme of intense family pain and a search for truth and justice.

"The first case is that of Noura Ghazi Safadi, a human rights lawyer, and Bassel Khartabil, an open-source developer," said Fedda. "In 2011 and 2012, they had become known as the 'newlyweds of the Syrian revolution'. The second one is that of the Italian priest Padre Paolo Dall'Oglio. The disappeared are Bassel and Paolo; the documentary's protagonists are Bassel's wife Noura and Paolo's sister Immacolata."

Noura and Immacolata cross paths in London for the first time after their fates had already become intertwined because of the political choices of their loved ones, the suffering of their wait and their stubborn search for truth. They share their story with the many other Syrian women who joined Families for Freedom, a movement which has been campaigning for justice since 2017.

The two women's stories seem to have found different endings, for now. Bassel and Noura met at a demonstration in the first two years of the Douma revolt against Bashar al-Assad's regime. They married while Bassel was held →

RIGHT: Bassel Khartabil and his wife Noura Ghazi Safadi. Khartabil disappeared from a prison cell and was executed by a Syrian army military court

→ at a prison in Adra, where Noura could still visit him. In 2015, Bassel (the 2013 Index award winner for digital freedom) disappeared from his cell and only after many years, after she moved to London, would Noura find out about his execution by a Syrian army military court, just a few months after his disappearance. But she has not yet been able to find out where the remains of her husband lie.

Paolo seems to have been taken prisoner by Isis in Raqqa in 2013 when he went to the militia's headquarters to negotiate the release of a kidnapped journalist with then-emir Abu Luqman. But according to testimony gathered by Italian journalist Amedeo Ricucci in Raqqa, he likely never got to speak with Luqman. He may not even have entered the Isis headquarters.

The main witness, Luqman, is still alive but has never made himself available, so there are no certainties about what happened to Paolo after the evening of his disappearance. Speculation abounds: he may have died in prison during the coalition bombing campaign against Isis; or his body may lie among thousands of others in one of the Raqqa's 26 mass graves for Isis victims. The two theories are two faces of the same coin: forced disappearances and mass imprisonment in Syria, at the hands of both the government and the various Islamist militias.

Fedda thinks the film could boost international calls for accountability.

"Forced disappearances in Syria are a huge issue that has largely remained outside international negotiations, whereas it should be central," she said. "Obtaining answers should be a priority. These families should be able to know what happened to their loved ones: if they have been killed, where they have been killed and where their bodies lie. Only through these trials could Syria be rebuilt tomorrow."

Although Noura has been able to find out the truth about what happened to Bassel – although it was a tragic discovery – the relatives of Paolo, who is fondly called "*abouna*" ("father") by his Syrian friends, are still in the dark. It was one of the reasons why Immacolata, or Machi, decided to be a protagonist and give a testimony in Fedda's documentary.

"Yasmin knew my brother for many years and had already started to make a film about his story in the monastery where he lived, in Mar Mousa in Syria," she said. "Then they met in Paris after al-Assad expelled him from Syria for his support of the revolution. Yasmin interviewed him, then Paolo decided to re-enter Syria with some rebels, and he disappeared in 2013.

"It was then that the idea of the film morphed into something new. Yasmin knew Noura in London and as the idea of telling the story of the disappeared in Syria grew, I thought that, sooner or later, I would have to speak publicly about it.

"I agreed to meet her in 2014 in Suleymania, in northern Iraq, where the community of Jesuits my brother belonged to has another monastery. And I opened up there. Years later,

I have to say Yasmin did me a big favour: it really helped me to process the disappearance, to deal with it, although the hope to hug my brother again remains always on my mind."

On 29 July this year, the Dall'Oglios called a press conference in Italy to take stock of the situation. Even if Paolo's remains lay in one of Raqqa's mass graves, Italian authorities never asked their Kurdish counterparts, who currently rule the region, to open an investigation into the matter. Why? Immacolata's words speak of a personal need but also of a collective one.

"We – I mean Noura and I – are small examples among thousands of people," she said. "And what has happened is a disgrace for humanity, on which there hasn't yet been enough attention. If one theory – not just for Paolo – is that there are so many mass graves for so many people whose names we do not have, it should be a collective duty to give these people a name.

"Giving these bodies a name and a surname would tell each story and helps us reconstruct the ways of history: to understand what has happened and who is responsible for it. Because sooner or later, history asks us who is responsible. Sooner or later, there are reckonings

in history. And this also applies to what has happened and is still happening in the regime's prisons. Here, too, sooner or later, history will demand a reckoning."

This reckoning has not yet happened: the stories of about 100 of the 100,000 victims swallowed in the darkness of this war appear on the side of a London bus that finishes the film Ayouni. Families for Freedom march on, from London to Berlin, to demand justice for their loved ones, coming from every city in Syria. The disappeared are men and women, young and old, students, doctors, teachers, developers, former soldiers.

They are united by one thing – they shared the courage to speak up against the censorship of the regime and the most violent militias because they dreamed of a free, plural, better Syria. ⊗

*Translated by **Alessio Perrone***

***Laura Silvia Battaglia** is a contributing editor at Index (Iraq and Yemen)*

ABOVE: Activists in Rome demand the release of Father Paolo Dall'Oglio, a Jesuit priest who was kidnapped in Syria in 2013. Dall'Oglio's whereabouts remain unknown

Blogger flees Tunisia after arrest

Layli Foroudi interviews a 27-year-old blogger who was punished for her atheism

49(03): 42/43 I DOI: 10.1177/0306422020958281

ONE NIGHT DURING lockdown in May, Tunisian blogger Emna Chargui posted some social-distancing advice on her Facebook page. Titled Sourat corona, it mimicked the embellishment of a religious text. At the time, she was sitting on the sofa next to her mother, Najat, a practising Muslim, who laughed. "I said to her, 'Emna! Always at it with the jokes. Stop!'"

Not everyone laughed. For the joke, Chargui was interrogated by seven prosecutors and sentenced to six months in prison for inciting hatred against religion. It wasn't just the content of the post that was up for discussion but her religious beliefs.

The 27-year-old is vocally atheist on her Facebook page, which has 25,000 followers and was given a blue tick on the day that we met in late July. She said: "They asked me, 'Are you atheist?' and when I said yes, they asked me, 'Do you take medication?' [and] 'Have you consulted a psychologist?'" Two weeks later, and after appealing her sentence, she left the country to live in Germany.

Questioning Chargui about her religious beliefs in this way was a violation of Article 6 of the constitution, which "guarantees freedom of conscience and belief", according to a political analyst and a former professor of law, who only wished to be referred to as Mohamed. "This demonstrates a social conservatism that is embodied by the judges, which is shared by the majority of Tunisians and by the world, in fact," he said. "It shows that there is a gap between the judges and the text."

"Charisma", a politician and businesswoman from the holy city of Kairouan, thinks the text itself is flawed. "The constitution is schizophrenic – there are parts where it accepts difference and parts where it does not," said the 36-year-old, who does not want to use her real name for security reasons.

In 2014, the first article was drafted ambiguously in a bid to satisfy both secular and Islamist sections of society, stating that "Tunisia is a civil state and Islam is its religion". Article 6, which guarantees freedom of belief, is itself ambivalent since it also "protects the sacred".

Since the 2000s, Tunisia has seen an increase in both secularism and religiosity, said Mohamed, with the latter given a boost in 2011 when the Islamist party Ennahdha was in power. A survey commissioned by the BBC found that Tunisians are increasingly identifying as "not religious" – 30% in 2018-19, twice as many as in 2013.

These twin dynamics became visible thanks to the freedom of expression gained after the 2011 revolution that toppled dictator Zine el Abidine Ben Ali. Art exhibitions on religion were hosted and films probing secularism were aired, but they attracted the ire of conservative Muslims. At the same time, secular civil society groups spoke of their religious compatriots with disdain. Opinions clashed and continue to clash, and the acceptance of difference is still

BELOW: Blogger Emna Chargui, who was sentenced to prison for a Facebook post

For the joke, Chargui was interrogated by seven prosecutors

elusive for many, whether religious or non-religious.

Freedom of expression has been a double-edged sword as these clashes are not always civil.

Khaled Maaref, a resident of the Beb Mnara neighbourhood in the Medina of Tunis, said that if we had met before 2011 he would have spoken to me, but in a whisper. "We had in our head that Ben Ali was everywhere," said the 56-year-old, who was warned by his Salafi neighbours that he should keep quiet for his safety. "I have more freedom to speak now, but I risk my life."

For Maaref, more freedom has meant more freedom for extremist religious groups, too. As a result, atheists are able to exercise their new-found freedom more so than before but so are Salafists and other groups, who are threatening those speaking out.

Perhaps the biggest factor in keeping atheist voices silent is a more banal social conservatism. Sitting with a group of friends in a cafe in the southern city of Gabès, Mohamed Lahssoumi, a 26-year-old with a construction business, tells me how he has been navigating Ramadan during the coronavirus lockdown. He discreetly eats bread and cheese in his bedroom, with the door closed.

"I can't talk about atheism with anyone here," he said, referring to his friends and speaking to me in English. "If you say you are atheist, they won't accept you – they insult atheists. People will say, 'Don't buy from that shop, he is an atheist'."

The same logic applies to politics. Charisma says that accepting the "non-religious" label would ruin her.

"They will not accept me into their region, into their home. They will judge me just by that and fight against me," she said. It would

hinder her work, she believes, since "the most important thing is to be close to people and see what they are suffering from, whether they are religious or not".

Maaref became persona non grata in two political parties – Afek Tounes and Mashrouu Tounes – because he always pushed the atheism issue. "They say [to me], 'We are for atheism and co-existence but it isn't the moment to speak about that, we need to wait'," he said.

Chargui's strategy is to speak. She had the right to refuse to answer the judge's question on her beliefs, but she relished the opportunity. "The goal is to show myself," she said. "If I don't then I risk living in a country that doesn't create laws for people [like me]. If we don't show ourselves, no one will know that we exist."

But she no longer lives in the country; she can speak only from afar. ⊗

Layli Foroudi is a freelance journalist based in Tunisia

Becoming tongue-tied

Sally Gimson reports on nations where they are attempting to wipe out minority languages

49(03): 44/46 I DOI: 10.1177/0306422020958282

PEOPLE ALL AROUND the world are in danger of losing their ability to speak in their native tongues, replaced by languages dictated by governments. But some are campaigning for them to be saved.

Unesco will launch its decade of indigenous languages in 2022, with the Los Pinos Declaration – signed in Mexico City – emphasising indigenous people's rights to freedom of expression, to an education in their mother tongues and to participation in public life using their own languages.

But while some are seeking to preserve languages, others are trying to wipe them out. In China's internment camps, Uighur Muslims are required to speak Mandarin rather than their native Turkic language. In a document published last year – The Fight Against Terrorism and Extremism and Human Rights Protection in Xinjiang – the Chinese government outlined its expectations of "trainees" in such camps.

Learning Mandarin is about "acquiring modern knowledge and information" and "adapting to contemporary society". Even Uighur families who are not in the camps are monitored to make sure they speak Mandarin – even in their own homes.

China is by no means the first nation to repress minority languages in a bid to crush a movement or a people. The practice is as old as language itself.

And as the world becomes more global and people travel more, dominant languages such as English, Mandarin, Hindi, Spanish and Arabic are pushing other, lesser-spoken, languages out.

Aurélie Joubert is a linguist who specialises in Occitan, the ancient lyrical language used by troubadours in medieval times. Although it is still spoken – mostly in southern France, but also in parts of Italy and Spain – it has been under threat for a long time.

Joubert believes that language loss is almost always down to politics when "one dominant culture takes over".

"Why? Well, politically, one group – the elite – speaks one language and dominates all the regions, so the languages spoken in those regions become less important."

The French language was used after the revolution to unite the country and get rid of the feudal system.

"It applies to a lot of countries. To unify a country politically, you try to impose a language on a national level," Joubert said.

Making everyone speak formal French was to "enlighten people" and give them, she added ironically, the "brilliance that is the French language". It became about expressing French national identity.

Regional languages were spoken only in private. And as communication increased and people became more mobile, leaving their villages to work in towns and cities, those languages died.

The introduction of the radio, said Joubert, meant that families began to listen to French and speak it at home, so languages such as Occitan were downgraded. Instead of being considered a proper language, it was referred to as a *patois* (a non-standard, provincial dialect) and became regarded as a sub-language, or barely a language at all.

And the more people tried to blend in, the more languages disappeared.

Losing languages means losing whole ways of thinking about the world and understanding it

"That affects people on a very personal level," said Joubert, who has interviewed many Occitan speakers for her research, "because you start losing your identity".

Until the 1950s, schools in France were forbidden to teach regional languages. They then became an "option", but were rarely taken up because of a lack of resources.

Corsican was missing from the list, ostensibly because it was too like Italian but in reality because of rising Corsican separatism.

In 2008, when regional languages were barely spoken at all, the government added Clause 75.1 to the French constitution, which said that "regional languages are part of the national heritage". But Article 2 of the constitution is clear. The language of the republic is French. And language guardian Académie Française polices the French language and decides usage, grammar and vocabulary.

The people responsible for wiping out many languages have been English speakers. Native languages on the American continent disappeared as native Americans were massacred by colonialists. Aboriginal languages have all but vanished in Australia due to colonisation – of the 250 in use in 1788 only 13 are still spoken by Australian children – and despite it's professed desire to support indigenous languages, there is pressure for indigenous people to speak English.

It is the only language taught in schools, and government documents are produced in English.

Some of the imposition of English has come about in the way Joubert describes the French experience: if you want to get on in the world, you have to speak English.

As a result, English is now spoken in more countries (101) than any other language, and there are more people learning English (1.5 billion) than are learning any other language.

But many developed countries have justified getting rid of indigenous languages and culture as being a religious "civilising" mission.

In Canada between 1863 and 1998, more than 150,000 indigenous children were taken from their families and sent to boarding schools run by religious authorities and the government. Children were not allowed to speak their own languages or practise their cultures. Many were abused and died. A Truth and Reconciliation report published in 2005 called it "cultural genocide". In 2019, the 2,800 children who had died in the homes were recognised for the first time and the National Centre for Truth and Reconciliation, in partnership with the Aboriginal People's Television Network, unveiled a national memorial.

Canada is now one of the countries working with Unesco on preserving the languages of Nisga'a and others trying to bring them back.

Mexico is doing something similar. It has the greatest linguistic diversity of anywhere in the world but – according to the National Institute of Indigenous Languages – hundreds of dialects are in danger of disappearing.

In the rest of Latin America, indigenous rights are closely linked to languages which are dying out. Even though there have been efforts to save them, and native languages are recognised, it is almost impossible to have a career or to fill in legal documents using those languages.

Jaco Du Toit, a Unesco chief of section, helped build the Unesco Atlas of the World's Languages in Danger, which has been renamed the World Atlas of Languages. It maps which languages are spoken around the world.

"Our strategy is to advocate for multilingualism and its importance in the development process," he said.

Unesco is also looking at novel ways to help keep languages alive, for example through →

ABOVE: A parade in the city of Bilbao in the Basque Country in 2011, part of the annual Semana Grande festival. The Basque Country straddles the border between Spain and France, and is home to people who traditionally speak the Basque language

SPAIN'S LONELY VOICES

Spanish minority languages are edging towards extinction, says SILVIA NORTES

"**A**S CHILDREN, MY** father and my uncle used to play a game where they slapped each other on the head and then they let out a word in Asturian," said Inaciu Galán, president of Iniciativa Pol Asturianu (Initiative for the Asturian Language), discussing how regional languages were "disappeared" during Franco's dictatorship. "Only Spanish was used at the school. That turned into self-repression in the family environment. Now, some old people do not want their grandchildren to speak Asturian, due to the bad perception instilled in them as children."

Spain's current constitution says Spanish is the official language of the state, and four co-official languages are also recognised: Catalan (in Catalonia), Galician (in Galicia), Euskera (in the Basque Country) and Aranese (in the Catalan Pyrenees). The last two, together with Aragonese and Astur-Leonese, are included in Unesco's Atlas of the World's Languages in Danger. But many more languages of Spain are struggling to survive, including Amazige, Fala, Ceuta Arabic and Romani.

Francisco Moscoso, a Ceuta Arabic researcher, says "this language is in a dangerous situation", since the administration promotes monolingualism and considers Ceuta Arabic to be "a non-traditional language of immigrants".

Meanwhile 38% of Aragonese users have stopped teaching it to their children, and the percentage of children who never speak Galician rose from 30% in 2008 to 44% in 2018.

The disappearance of a culture is intimately linked to the disappearance of its language. Many words refer to animals, plants or traditional trades. María Sánchez, a well-known writer, collects these words in her book Almáciga. "It's not just words but sustainable production models. And sounds: we no longer know the sound of a cart on the cobblestones or the wheel of an old mill," she told Ethic magazine.

In Unesco's words, "increased migration and urbanisation often bring along the loss of traditional ways of life and a pressure to speak a dominant language that is – or is perceived to be – necessary for economic advancement". This was Aranese's case. The opening of the Vielha tunnel in the Catalan Pyrenees in 1948 brought in tourists and workers from other parts of Spain, which made Spanish the main mother tongue of the area. In 2018, Spanish had become the initial language for 38% of the population while Aranese was for 21%.

The exodus to cities in the second half of the 20th century also made minority languages in rural areas more vulnerable. Most of the speakers of Estremeñu in Extremadura are aged 60 or older. However, associations are emerging to preserve languages and their cultures, such as Nogará Cultural Association, which has been teaching courses in Aragonese for 25 years. Hispanist Beatrice Bottin highlights the case of Basque culture, which uses language as an integrating element through *bertsolarismo*, tournaments where poets improvise verses in Euskera.

→ digital empowerment. And the First Peoples' Cultural Council in Canada has already developed dictionary apps to revitalise indigenous languages across several countries.

Du Toit says losing languages means losing whole ways of understanding the world. Some languages, he says, have different words for different clouds, and those symbolic words, with their nuanced description of how the clouds behave, might help us save crops.

For Joubert, the disappearance of languages is like climate change and, in the same way, what is happening is intrinsically political.

"The link between the two is the respect of natural habitat. It's maybe more obvious for climate change – for instance, lakes – but for language it happens when you purposefully, or not, destroy communities. That means a language does not have its natural habitat." ⊗

Sally Gimson is a freelance journalist and writer based in London

Even Uighur families who are not in the camps are monitored to make sure they speak Mandarin

Why Index has never been needed more

The non-stop oppression of freedom around the world means the work of Index is as important as ever, says incoming chief executive **Ruth Smeeth**

49(03): 48/49 I DOI: 10.1177/0306422020958284

THERE ARE MOMENTS in life that force us to take a step back and consider who we are and what we want to achieve – those moments that beg the question: what is really important to us? Which battles are we willing to fight? They cause us to examine and confront what drives us and who we each want to be.

I think every one of us has had at least one of those moments in 2020 as we've seen almost too much news – too many things that have touched our hearts or made us angry.

In recent months, the world has been dominated by Covid-19 – a virus that none of us had heard of this time last year but which, as of mid-August, has now killed more than 735,000 people globally and infected more than 20 million. Those are just the official statistics. In reality, we have no idea how many people have actually died, untested and alone.

But what we do know is that some governments have chosen this pandemic as cover to restrict free speech and attack our basic human rights. According to Index's disease control tracker, there have been more than 240 incidents in which the premise of protecting public health has been used to curtail freedom of expression.

We've seen the global impact of the Black Lives Matter movement which, after years of demanding change, came to rightly dominate the news agenda after the horrendous killing of George Floyd. It has inspired a new generation of equality campaigners and forced all of us to reflect on what really matters. The loss and pain of so many has made us think about what social justice can and should look like in the 21st century. It has widened the debate about how we should all reflect on our history.

In July, we saw investigative journalism at its best when the story of Uighur Muslims and the horrifying events in Xinjiang finally got the global attention it deserved. The appalling actions of the Chinese government have been exposed. The world has watched the Uighur people transported to "re-education camps", we've heard the stories of family members being disappeared, and we've seen the piles of hair believed to have been forcibly cut in images reminiscent of the Holocaust.

The charge sheet against the Chinese government is ever growing. Beijing has made significant moves against the residents of Hong Kong with the national security law, instigating a new regime that is completely at odds with the spirit and letter of the Sino-British Joint Declaration. Campaigners, journalists and people of faith have been arrested without cause, media outlets have been raided and books have been removed from libraries. The thought police have moved in and their targets are those who speak out.

But China is not alone in seeking to roll back the freedoms of thought and expression that go hand in glove with a functioning democracy. The totalitarian actions of Alexander Lukashenko in Belarus, with his farcical election and the deployment of the military to quell the protests, are the latest in a long line of worrying developments which put free

---

The loss and pain of so many has made us think about what social justice can and should look like in the 21st century

speech at risk. Consider, too, Narendra Modi's government in India, with its revocation of Article 370 last year and the repressive lockdown faced by the residents of Jammu and Kashmir, as well as the troubling development in Poland, where Andrzej Duda was re-elected on an alt-right populist ticket which seeks to scapegoat and marginalise those who dissent or wish to protect their freedom.

Collectively, we have so much to be angry and worried about – and that's before we start to reflect on the latest actions of Donald Trump, Jair Bolsonaro, Vladimir Putin and Benjamin Netanyahu, and dozens of othern leaders who apparently view their accumulation of personal power as the sole objective of government.

Each of these issues has a clear connection: without journalistic freedoms, without our rights to free speech and association, and without social media platforms and global news coverage, we simply wouldn't know about them.

We wouldn't know about Merdan Ghappar, currently incarcerated in an Uighur camp. We wouldn't know about the arrest of Wilson Li, the ITV freelancer, in Hong Kong and we wouldn't know the name of George Floyd. The fact that we do reminds us again of the power of our collective voices and how much we need to cherish and protect our rights to use them.

That is why I am so proud to be the new chief executive of Index on Censorship and to help lead that fight. Index was launched nearly 50 years ago to provide a voice for the persecuted and to shine a light on the actions of repressive regimes. We have fought numerous battles in the last half-century, but if the past few months have taught us anything it's that we still have many more fights ahead, and your voice and that of Index has never been more needed or more important.

The appalling actions of the Chinese government have been exposed

In the coming months, the team and I want to work with you as we redouble our efforts to ensure that this magazine and our organisation are fit and ready for the fights ahead, and that we are using every tool at our disposal to shine a spotlight on governments that for too long have been able to hide in the dark.

This year has been a heart-breaking one for too many families in every part of the world. Index was established originally to provide a home and some hope for Soviet dissidents and others who no longer believed that anybody was listening to them. My promise to you is that Index will continue this tradition and be a bastion of hope for those people leading the fight against repression; for those who struggle to have their voices heard and their experiences recognised; and, of course, for those whose names we don't yet know – but will. ⊗

ABOVE: Hong Kong protesters leave their mark on the streets in the city

Ruth Smeeth *is CEO of Index on Censorship*

MAIN: A lone Trump supporter at a re-election campaign rally in Tulsa, USA in June. The rally had much lower attendance numbers than Trump's staff had expected

IN FOCUS

Ecce homo sovieticus

Freedoms are slowly being eroded as the Russian government tightens its grip. But not everyone seems to be noticing, writes
Andrey Arkhangelsky

49(03): 52/55 I DOI: 10.1177/0306422020958285

OVER THE PAST 20 years, the main aim of the Russian authorities has been clear: the gradual dismantling of democracy. They have gone about eroding all the key aspects of a free society and the end result is that, today, Russia is a huge social laboratory.

In it, we can see how the virus of totalitarianism lives on, even after the collapse of the USSR. "Homo sovieticus continues to reproduce" was the main conclusion reached in 1994 by the oldest Russian sociological organisation, the Levada Centre (which, since 2017, has been dubbed a "foreign agent").

Why do most people in Russia agree to the restriction of their freedoms? There could be several reasons.

One could be the problem of all "revolutions from above".

In 1985, President Mikhail Gorbachev began his policy of *perestroika* (restructuring) and gave people political freedom, which led to the victory of the bourgeois revolution in 1991.

But it was only the minority who benefitted from the economic reforms. The majority blamed democracy for all their problems.

Another is that the main criterion of the "totalitarian character" (as defined in Autoritäre Persönlichkeit, a study by Theodor W Adorno) is the absence of self-awareness: post-Soviet people do not consider themselves to be independent personalities.

They have never separated themselves from the collective body of the state, and the high level of education and culture – of which Russia is so proud – has in no way altered people's consciousness. They have not grown used to making their own decisions about their freedoms or about their rights, continuing to entrust fundamental decisions to the state.

And then there is the fact that the erosion of freedoms in Russia has coincided with the growth of populism throughout the world. But in Russian society, unlike that in the USA or Europe, there is no immunity from state violence. Homo sovieticus doesn't consider the disappearance of his rights and freedoms to be a threat to his very existence.

Nevertheless, as events of the last few years have demonstrated, the basic instincts of democracy are still alive in Russia, too.

The chief driving force of protest today is young people who have lived all their lives under President Vladimir Putin. But instincts have been reawakened in older people who experienced *perestroika*.

This July, Khabarovsk – in Russia's far east – saw the start of the largest protests to have taken place in the last 20 years. People are angry about the arrest of the local governor, Sergei Furgal, and are demanding *glasnost* (openness) in the investigation. This is another common slogan from the Gorbachev era.

The biggest protests in the regions may be linked to ecology (as in the town of Shies) or anti-clericalism (as in Yekaterinburg), but what unites them is the battle for a sense of personal dignity. Protesters in Russia are now demanding respect as well as dialogue with the authorities. But the regime is, on principle, unable to engage: in the Kremlin this would be seen as a sign of weakness.

So the Kremlin itself is provoking increasing dissatisfaction. We can describe the protests →

In the minds of the secret services, a journalist can be either the Kremlin's assistant or its enemy

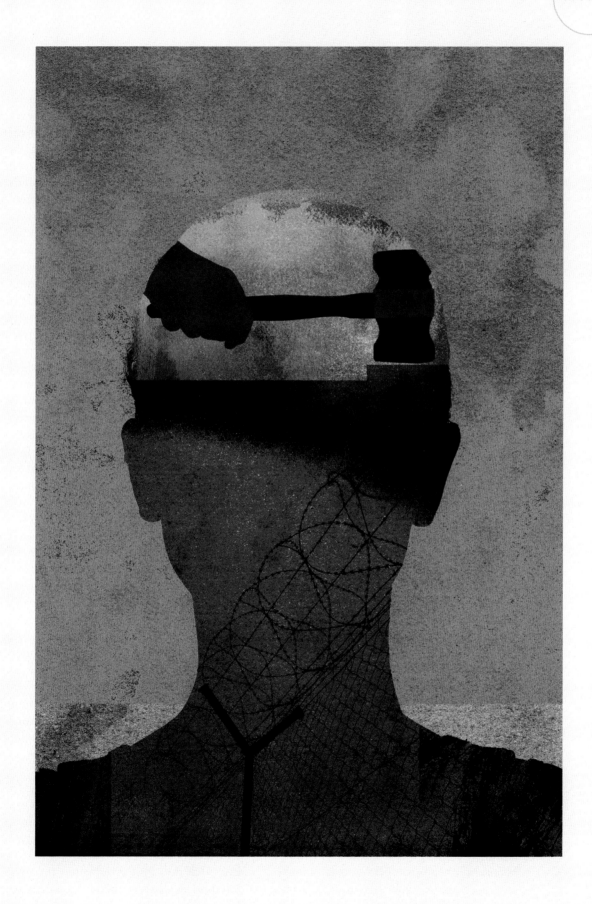

→ that are happening today in Russia as "moral". But for now, moral protest has not become political protest. (The only protests we can call "political" are those in Moscow and St Petersburg, but it is only a minority who support them.)

The process of disappearing public freedom began, many would argue, with the near-elimination of independent television and the loss of the NTV and TVS TV companies in 2002-2003. The only independent channel left today is cable channel Dozhd.

After the terrorist attack on a school in Beslan in 2003, Putin abolished direct elections for regional governors. A new wave of restrictions on freedom began in 2012, following the first demonstrations during Putin's time in office, which protested about alleged rigging of the elections to the state Duma.

The political opposition continues to come under constant pressure. All public gatherings or demonstrations must be approved in advance – despite the Russian constitution, as before, guaranteeing freedom of assembly – and two or more people gathering are threatened with legal proceedings.

Repressive laws have also been passed: "on forbidding the propagation of ideas about non-traditional sexual orientation" (2013); and on "undesirable organisations" and "foreign agents" (2014). These restrict the activities of human rights and civil society organisations and encourage discrimination against members of the LGBTQ community.

In 2019, parliament passed a law making it possible to exclude the Russian part of the internet from the rest of the world (the so-called "Chinese variation"), as well as imposing control over social media messaging. More and more, we hear about the secret services torturing people who have been accused of crimes or are under suspicion, such as the case of the youth organisation Set (Network), which was accused of being involved in terrorism.

In 2020, the very principle of being able to change the elected authorities has been smashed. After the alterations made to the constitution, Putin can stand for election again in 2024, and could rule the country until 2036.

Furthermore, all elections will now take place over the course of three days. This new procedure creates huge possibilities for falsifying the results and the changes represent the last step in removing any legitimacy from elections in Russia.

The main aim of any authoritarian regime is survival. But when that regime begins to feel its strength, it goes on the attack. Other recent populist changes to the constitution, introduced in July, can now be used as repressive measures and represent a ban on freedom of thought.

Freedom of speech is suffering most. Over the past 10 years, dozens of independent publications have closed because pressure has been put on their owners. Now they are going after individual journalists.

In 2018, Svetlana Prokopyeva, a journalist from Pskov, was accused of inciting terrorism in an article she wrote about an explosion in the FSB reception hall. She was recently given a suspended sentence and a fine.

Most often they go after those engaged in investigative journalism. In July 2018, Orkhan Dzhemal, a journalist specialising in military affairs, Alexander Rastorguev, a producer, and their cameraman, Kirill Radchenko, were shot dead while they were investigating the activities of private Russian military company the Wagner Group in the Central African Republic.

While those who carried out the killings are as yet unknown, independent experts have shown that these murders were carefully planned and carried out.

In 2019, Ivan Golunov, an investigative journalist at the Meduza publishing house, was accused of drug-dealing. Only after a public protest was he found not guilty and released.

In the summer of 2020, former journalist Ivan Safronov – now an adviser to the head of the Russian space agency – was accused of espionage. Specialists consider that these cases have all been brought as acts of revenge because of the individuals' professional activities.

And it is often those engaged in independent professions who are the targets of such cases. In 2020, theatre director Kirill Serebrennikov was found guilty of embezzling state funds in a case he maintains was politically motivated. It dragged on for three years, and he received a six-year suspended sentence and a massive fine.

Late in 2019, a case was opened against artist Yulia Tsvetkova (also this year's Index arts award winner) for her drawings in a series she called The Vagina Monologues. She could receive up to six years imprisonment.

Finally, there is the widely publicised case of human rights activist Yury Dmitriev, who was uncovering the names of people who had been shot during Stalin's Terror. The court accused him of paedophilia and eventually handed him a three-and-a-half-year prison sentence.

The leadership in the Kremlin (there can be no doubt that these serious cases are all controlled by the highest authority) continue to live in the past, in the world of Soviet dogma. In their view of the world, there is no place for people wanting to lead their own lives.

The Kremlin simply cannot comprehend that people may have their own principles, convictions or goals. It cannot understand that a person may wish to uphold the truth rather than another's particular interests.

There was no place for a profession such as "investigative journalist" in the USSR, and they do not see that such a profession can be part of the fabric of society now. In the minds of the secret services, a journalist can be either the Kremlin's assistant or its enemy.

All these processes are not simply about the pursuit of certain individuals. They are bringing a charge against democracy itself. They don't like "abstract ideas" in the Kremlin, such as the kind of social structure we have now in Russia.

They prefer the situational ethic (just do what's convenient now) and rhetoric (you can justify any action with the use of the right words). But this hybrid of values leads to a lack of an adequate response even to their own actions. In this way the Kremlin is creating yet another historical experiment: it is trying to create a synthesis of democracy and totalitarianism, of freedom and slavery.

In this, much depends on the psychology of Putin himself. Probably up to a certain point he was a supporter of what was modern; at least, while it referred only to technology. But when the individual uses this modernity for the sake of progress, it becomes a nightmare for the Kremlin.

But there is one thing we can say for sure: the "era of stability" (economic stability in exchange for civil freedoms), which has been the main foundation of post-Soviet authoritarian regimes, is coming to an end. The authoritarian regime has ceased to be effective economically, and the pandemic has hastened this process. The authorities are aware of their weaknesses, which is why they are becoming more aggressive.

The most surprising thing is that the new ethic which is coming from the West is also changing post-Soviet people and a new battle is beginning in the post-Soviet space.

It is a battle for what will be considered the norm in the years ahead. The law or lawlessness? Freedom or madness? A life in which there is a place for the individual or one in which all is subsumed by the totalitarian state?

For now, at least, all is not lost. ⊗

*Translated by **Stephen Dalziel***

***Andrey Arkhangelsky** is a writer and columnist based in Moscow, Russia*

"I have suffered death threats and they killed my pet dogs"

Index's **Stephen Woodman** finds Mexican reporters struggling with higher levels of psychological disorders than war correspondents

49(03): 56/59 I DOI: 10.1177/0306422020958286

DURING SLEEPLESS NIGHTS at his home in Ciudad Obregón, northern Mexico, Marco Antonio Duarte wonders whether the people who destroyed his car will come back to take his life.

The 59-year-old journalist suspects that a government official was behind the firebombing of his vehicle in May, which was just the latest in a series of aggressions that have left him in a state of constant anxiety.

"You try to be strong," Duarte told Index. "But I have suffered physical damage [and] death threats, people have robbed me, and they have killed my pet dogs."

Campaign groups are calling for greater investment in the treatment of psychological problems in the lead-up to World Mental Health Day on 10 October. But few Mexican media outlets provide care for the reporters at the frontline of the nation's security crisis – even though they work in the deadliest country for the press in the western hemisphere.

At least 133 media workers have lost their lives because of their reporting in Mexico since 2000.

That figure includes Jorge Armenta, a close friend of Duarte's, who was shot dead as he left a restaurant in Ciudad Obregón in May. And unknown assailants killed journalist José Luis Castillo in the same city in June.

Besides dealing with the loss of colleagues to violence, Mexican journalists routinely suffer threats and physical aggression. While the exact emotional toll of such an environment is impossible to quantify, trauma research points to acute levels of psychological distress.

One recent review of 35 studies on the emotional well-being of media workers from around the world concluded that "rates of psycho-pathology among journalists appear to be higher than in the general population". Increased exposure to potentially traumatic events and poor social support were both risk factors for greater distress.

In 2012, neuropsychiatrist Dr Anthony Feinstein published one of the few studies focused on Mexican media workers.

He observed alarming rates of post-traumatic stress disorder, anxiety and depression among the sample. Feinstein also found a quarter of the journalists he studied had stopped covering stories because of intimidation.

Drug cartels had managed to "undermine the freedom of the press", Feinstein told Index. "The media were being manipulated through fear."

In a follow-up analysis published in 2013, Feinstein concluded that Mexican journalists working in dangerous areas had even more symptoms suggestive of psychological disorders than war correspondents did.

"The typical conflict reporter flies into a war zone for three or four weeks and returns

OPPOSITE: Forensics inspect the body of someone who tried to steal the vehicle of journalist Hector de Mauleon in Mexico City, May 2019

to their country of origin," Feinstein said. "But [Mexican journalists] don't have the option to go back to recouperate and recharge their batteries. There is no such downtime for this group. They are living in very dangerous areas, doing extremely dangerous work."

Feinstein also observed that fear for the safety of family members was the "single biggest factor undermining [the journalists'] ability to do their work".

Duarte told Index that concerns for his wife's physical and psychological wellbeing were the main source of his own distress.

There were clandestine graves and, from 2017, bodies began to appear hanging in public places

Both are receiving counselling as part of Mexico's Mechanism to Protect Human Rights Defenders and Journalists. Established in 2012, this manages the safeguarding of more than 1,000 people.

→ Given the level of risk Duarte faces, the programme has offered to move him to a safe house in another city. But he has refused, as he worries his tormentors will destroy his home in his absence. He says moving would also deprive him and his wife of a support network of friends and colleagues.

According to Diego Martinez, a human rights lawyer who has represented at-risk journalists, the mechanism does little to address the impact of trauma on freedom of expression.

"The specific aim of moving journalists … is to offer them physical protection," he said. "But in protection mechanism meetings, mental

There is no such downtime for this group. They are living in very dangerous areas, doing extremely dangerous work

health solutions are rarely discussed."

While Martinez is not pushing for the removal of safe houses from the programme, he is calling for greater consideration and investment in the emotional impact of attacks. By only protecting physical wellbeing, Martinez says the relocation scheme generates other issues for victims.

"When journalists completely change their lives because of a specific traumatic event … they have to get used to a new environment and to not seeing friends or family," he said. "They also have to stay in the shelter most of the time, sometimes without the possibility of leaving."

Gladys Navarro, a reporter for El Universal newspaper, believes the Covid-19 pandemic has compounded the existing mental health crisis for Mexican media workers. She points to health fears, the stresses of social distancing and increased job insecurity as the principal sources of strain.

Navarro lives in the coastal state of Baja California Sur, which had avoided the drug gang violence that rocked other parts of the country. "Crime reporting used to focus on car accidents, fights, robberies; crimes of that nature," she said.

In July 2014, a cartel shootout in the state capital La Paz marked the beginning of a wave of murder that swept across the peninsula, and the press had to function in a deeply traumatic environment.

"Crime reporters had to cover high-impact crimes: executions and dismembered bodies … There were clandestine graves and, from 2017, bodies began to appear hanging in public places."

Although the crime rate has declined in the past two years, the emotional consequences of the outbreak linger. "Many journalists suffer chronic insomnia and anxiety disorders," Navarro said. "There was no training or support... We went out without any of that."

Navarro said the experience had fostered a culture of solidarity among reporters in the state. They have since developed security protocols, formed a collective and organised protests. But access to counselling remains limited. Navarro has been in therapy for a year, covering the cost herself as no organisation or government body has offered to pay for the treatment.

In recent years, freedom of expression groups such as Article 19, Periodistas de a Pie and the Dart Centre for Journalism and Trauma have offered counselling and mental health workshops to Mexican media workers.

And Noroeste, a newspaper based in the troubled Pacific state of Sinaloa, is one of the few media outlets in the country to offer free psychological support to staff as a permanent option.

"We decided to hire a psychologist because we realised there was still this false idea that if you felt vulnerable, you couldn't handle the job," said Adrián López, Noroeste's director general.

"We don't have access to any information on who visits [the psychologist], nor do we refer people to them. We just insist our editors let everyone know the resource is there."

In some parts of the country, such as the border state of Tamaulipas, the drug cartels and corrupt officials have won. Investigative journalists have fallen silent, unable to report on their surroundings for fear of violent retaliation.

The predicament illustrates the threat that a traumatic landscape poses – both to individual journalists and to journalism itself.

López believes the failure to provide adequate psychological support to staff was a major factor driving the freedom of expression crisis across Mexico and represents a significant moral failing of the industry. According to him, cost concerns are the main reason managers refuse to add psychologists to the payroll. But he argues that therapeutic interventions make sense, even in purely economic terms.

"It would be more expensive to lose a journalist because they burn out or abandon their passion and discipline. All that is more expensive," López said. "It can be difficult to sustain these policies, but it's always cheaper to have a stable organisation." ⊗

ABOVE: Marco Antonio Duarte, whose car was bombed back in May

Stephen Woodman is Index's contributing editor for Mexico, based in Guadalajara

Nonsense and sensibility

Bestselling author **Dave Eggers** tells **Jemimah Steinfeld** why he thinks we are losing the battle to protect our own privacy and will end up with a completely surveilled society

49(03): 60/62 I DOI: 10.1177/0306422020958287

FINDING THE RIGHT words to express himself is not a problem you'd associate with Dave Eggers. The award-winning author of many books, Eggers often tackles the thorniest social issues of the day. And yet, when it comes to the current political situation in his home country, the USA, he is struggling.

"We're living through a period of such lunacy that it can't be described without one's head exploding," he told Index.

Still, he gives it a bash.

"Here in the USA, the Republican party has lived in a parallel universe of highly refracted truth for some time," he said.

"They manufactured the war in Iraq based on wholly fabricated information, and they got away with it. Since then, there has been no significant inquiry about the war, and not one American lost their job over an unjust war that cost about a million Iraqi lives."

The situation has become much worse due to Covid-19. Eggers says that the level of "incompetence at work here is breathtaking" and even though many would have died irrespective of leadership, "the current misinformation campaign related to the virus, coupled with weak and dithering leadership," is definitely part of it.

"The GOP's indifference to truth, science and common sense has made possible an extremely reckless and radical agenda for a party that had heretofore been known as 'conservative'."

At the same time as the Republicans might be undercutting truth, our privacy is being eroded

– a topic Eggers is particularly concerned about.

He broke into the literary scene in 2000 with his first book, A Heartbreaking Work of Staggering Genius, a partly fictionalised memoir of losing both his parents to cancer when he was 21 and having to then raise his younger brother.

But it was The Circle that turned Eggers into a household name. Released in 2013, it was a time when "Google it" was a firmly established term and stories of the endless perks of working at Google's California headquarters filled column inches. Eggers imagined a Google-type company whose well-meaning idea to connect the world takes a very sinister turn. It was based on aspects of the present, but was also a projection of the future.

"I was trying to scare myself," Eggers said of the writing process.

"I envisioned a few dozen developments that I found terrifying but not 100% likely. But, then, so many of those things happened within months of the book being published. I thought I was projecting some near-ludicrous scenarios that might happen 10 years out, but instead they unfolded in weeks.

"The core of my fear, and the factor that's driving us into a near-total panopticon of our own making, is that no one cares in any real way about privacy, and that the right to know will always trample the right to privacy.

"That drives most of the more nefarious innovations of the last 20 years and will continue to drive us towards a society of total surveillance and zero privacy. It's a fast-running river that can't be turned back."

Eggers says it's "nearly impossible" to find a company with "any innate sense of boundaries".

No one cares in any real way about privacy

TOP RIGHT: The author Dave Eggers

No one – neither corporation nor consumer – cares to set them.

"No one reads the small print, and the small print changes daily, and daily we're presented with 10 new implicit or explicit contracts, all containing small print," he said. "It's too much to track.

"In general, I really do believe that people on the whole see the collection of data as an inherent good. The collection of data recently, to track the movement of people during Covid-19, is universally seen as helpful. But it's all done without anyone's consent. Governments and corporations are taking note of the utter lack of resistance."

Eggers believes that there will be an exponential increase in data collection without consent over the next five years. This is based in part on our response, or lack thereof, to data collection so far.

"I haven't seen much outrage in the last 20 years," he said. "There is, instead, a brief roll of the eyes at every new privacy violation."

This must irk him, and yet he's remarkably understanding and non-judgemental.

"I personally use all kinds of tech that is inherently exploitive and privacy-trampling, and it's always driven by expedience and convenience," he said.

I haven't seen much outrage in the last 20 years. There is, instead, a brief roll of the eyes at every new privacy violation

→ Many of us in Western democracies, Eggers says, are lucky to have not experienced "the truly nefarious outcomes from surveillance".

"We don't have so many examples of police knocking down doors and arresting people en masse due to warrantless surveillance. There are some cases that fit that profile, but not so many. In general, we're just changing from one species into another. Twenty years ago, we valued privacy as an inherent right and necessity. That principle will be largely gone in our lifetimes."

Eggers, whose background also includes writing a comic strip and running a magazine, has written often of the importance and value of non-digital, analogue lives. Is that aspect becoming more dream than reality?

"In our lifetimes, cash will largely be abolished and nearly all media will be experienced via digital means," he said. "There are no powerful interests that stand to gain by defending analogue living. We should not have to have smartphones and laptops to get an education, interact with our government, or vote. But increasingly, in the interests of cost-savings and efficiency, democracy will be accessed only through screens and digital means."

For Eggers, this is not just a shame. He believes, damningly, that "it'll make us far less interesting as a species".

The Covid-19 pandemic, with its associated restrictions, has accelerated this negative trend and Eggers highlights online schooling, which has been carried out during lockdown.

"Even 10 years ago, teachers during a pandemic might have said, 'read a chapter of this book each day, and let's talk at the end of the week'. Now there is this never-severed digital tether, and children are on their screens eight to 10 hours a day... It works against a child's sense of daily balance and diversity of experience. Even in terms of physical education, children in the USA are required to send their phys-ed teachers videos of them exercising. It's loony."

Despite his concerns, Eggers is still positive. Indeed, he is a firm believer in the over-riding good of humanity.

In addition to his own writing, Eggers is co-founder of 826 National, a network of youth writing and tutoring centres, as well as ScholarMatch, a non-profit organisation designed to connect students with resources, schools and donors to make college possible for those from low-income backgrounds.

He also runs McSweeney's, a non-profit publishing company with a mission statement of championing "ambitious and inspired new writing" and challenging "conventional expectations about where it's found, how it looks, and who participates". A publishing house to help others, at this stage McSweeney's appears to be a tonic for Eggers.

"I've been editing a lot of short essays lately by two groups – healthcare workers and citizens over 60. These are two platforms we started on the McSweeney's website. Every day, we post a few short essays and, I have to say, hearing directly from so many people, most of them non-professional writers, has been a balm," he said.

"People are so good. When you take time to listen to them they are gorgeous and brave."

He jokes that this positivity is at odds with the cynical take of the rest of the interview – and, perhaps, with the works he is most widely known for – but for Eggers, all is not ultimately lost.

"The truth is that I think we still have options," he said. "We can, for the time being, make choices that give us more control and balance in our lives. We just need the will to make those choices. The will is everything." ⊗

Jemimah Steinfeld is deputy editor at Index on Censorship

Fighting the laws that are silencing journalists

A new Index report calls for measures, including an anti-Slapp directive, to be put in place to protect journalists from vexatious legal threats and actions, writes **Jessica Ní Mhainín**

49(03): 63/65 I DOI: 10.1177/0306422020958288

AT THE TIME of her assassination in 2017, Maltese journalist Daphne Caruana Galizia was facing 47 civil and criminal defamation suits. After her death, about 30 of these were transferred to her family under a Maltese law that allows claimants to pursue actions against the heirs of a deceased defendant.

Caruana Galizia is among the most well-known targets in Europe. Slapps – an acronym for strategic lawsuits against public participation – are a type of legal action not undertaken to be won but to intimidate defendants into silence or inaction. They are most often used by powerful actors (corporations, public officials, high-profile businesspeople) in an attempt to stop individuals or organisations from expressing critical views on issues of public interest. They imperil not only independent journalism but academia, activism and other forms of civic engagement. And they seem to be becoming more common around the world.

"Free speech is vastly protected by the anti-Slapp statute – it's a night and day difference," said California-based lawyer Thomas R Burke about a law in the USA that protects people from being vexatiously sued for exercising their right to free speech. Burke was speaking at a roundtable event organised by Index in July. He was one of 15 legal practitioners and academics to have participated in a virtual discussion which forms the basis for Breaking the Silence, a report published by Index this week that looks at the legal measures that will help give journalists back their voices. It is the second report from Index on Censorship's ongoing research project into Slapps following our May report that looked in depth at the legal challenges journalists are facing in countries across Europe.

"Even though we know that they will win, it still takes several years," said one participant regarding vexatious criminal lawsuits in Hungary. Slapps are usually based on defamation laws, and can take the form of criminal lawsuits when national laws permit. Lengthy litigation is characteristic of Slapp lawsuits, with plaintiffs typically looking to drain defendants of as much time and money as possible in an effort to punish them and discourage any further scrutiny. Excessively strict defamation laws and lengthy judicial procedures are just two of the issues that are amplifying the impact of Slapps, according to Breaking the Silence.

In the Breaking the Silence report lawyers in Hungary, Poland and Northern Ireland have expressed concern over the increasing misuse of the EU's General Data Protection Regulation and privacy laws. According to the new report, police in the Polish city of Olsztyn issued a statement earlier this year saying that publishing videos of police interventions online "may give rise to liability for violation of the provisions on the protection of personal data". Poland's commissioner for human ⟶

Civil society and the media must come together to ensure that journalists are supported and are not silenced

→ rights condemned the misleading statement and called on Olsztyn police to amend it who referred to GDPR's journalistic exemption, which also applies to citizen journalists.

Breaking the Silence also puts forward some potential recommendations that could impede the effectiveness of Slapps, as discussed by the legal experts who attended the roundtable. One of the most far-reaching measures is the introduction of anti-Slapp legislation, such as an EU anti-Slapp directive. Věra Jourová, the EU commissioner for values and transparency,

has indicated that she is in favour of this. In June, she replied to MEPs who had written to her about this saying she would look at "all possible options to address this matter".

The right to privacy is protected under Article 8 of the European Convention on Human Rights, and freedom of expression may be subject to restrictions if anyone's privacy is unlawfully interfered with. Legislation would need to respect individuals' rights to bring legitimate action against any violation of these rights, while also offering increased

There's rather a tendency to restrict and repress

protection to journalists, activists and others who speak out on matters of public interest.

What could such legislation look like? Breaking the Silence includes the insights of Burke, who has successfully litigated hundreds of anti-Slapp cases in California – a state that has had an anti-Slapp statute in place since 1992. According to Burke, the statute enables a defendant to file a motion to dismiss complaints through a quick judgment-like procedure. Once the motion is filed, amendments cannot be made to the complaint and the plaintiff cannot dismiss it without facing legal fees. The motion also places a freeze on discovery (pre-trial exchange of evidence), the most expensive stage of litigation in the USA. If the motion is granted, the action is dismissed and the defendant recovers all costs.

"It would be enormously effective, but how do we do that now when we have politicians banging on about fake news?" replied one of the European lawyers upon hearing of the legislation. As Breaking the Silence shows, several of legal experts expressed concern about the prospect of introducing such legislation amid the current political environment. "Politicians are very reluctant at the moment to give additional protections to online media and social media. There's rather a tendency to restrict and repress," noted one legal expert.

As efforts continue among a coalition of civil society organisations – which includes Index on Censorship – to push for an EU anti-Slapp directive, other measures can be put in place to help support Slapp victims. Among the measures proposed in Breaking the Silence are training for judges and journalists, a rethink of the role of the jury in media trials, and the full application of European Court of Human Rights (ECtHR) case law.

Norway, which has comparatively few Slapp cases, is mentioned as an example. "In the 1980s and 1990s, defamation cases were a problem – a big problem – for the Norwegian press because we had not incorporated properly the jurisprudence of the European Court," explained one Norwegian lawyer. Now Norwegian courts allow for defences provided for by ECtHR jurisprudence to be used. "It doesn't mean the media don't lose cases," he said, "but it's a much more realistic attitude toward press freedom."

According to Breaking the Silence, another reason why Norway has been so successful in protecting its media against Slapps is the well-organised nature of its editors' and press associations. This contrasts with Italy, where the media – and freelance journalists in particular – are habitually targeted with Slapps. According to Italian lawyer Andrea di Pietro, who spoke to Index, "journalists are really economically isolated, also from a trade union perspective; therefore, weakening journalists with a lawsuit is very possible thanks to a legal system that doesn't punish [the vexatious litigators]".

The implementation of Breaking the Silence's recommendations will be key to protecting freedom of expression and democracy. But some recommendations – not least the introduction of anti-Slapp legislation – will take time to bring about. In the meantime, civil society and the media must come together to ensure that journalists are supported and are not silenced by these abusive legal threats and actions. ⊗

Jessica Ní Mhainín is senior policy research and advocacy officer at Index

A new report on the legal measures that will give journalists back their voices

X index the voice of free expression

ABOVE: The second of our series of Index reports from our ongoing research into Slapps

Jennings

2020 BY BEN JENNINGS

ALEXA, GIVE US THE HEADLINES

HOSTILITIES BETWEEN THE US AND IRAN HAVE INCREASED AFTER PRESIDENT TRUMP ORDERED A DRONE STRIKE...

ALEXA — HEADLINES PLEASE

WILDFIRES CONTINUE TO BURN THROUGH AUSTRALIA...

...MEANWHILE, THE UK HAS SEEN SEVERE FLOODING AS IT PREPARES TO OFFICIALLY WITHDRAW FROM THE EU

ALEXA, CAN I GET TODAY'S NEWS

SIGH

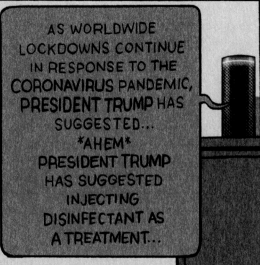

AS WORLDWIDE LOCKDOWNS CONTINUE IN RESPONSE TO THE CORONAVIRUS PANDEMIC, PRESIDENT TRUMP HAS SUGGESTED... *AHEM* PRESIDENT TRUMP HAS SUGGESTED INJECTING DISINFECTANT AS A TREATMENT...

49(03): 66/67 I DOI: 10.1177/0306422020958289

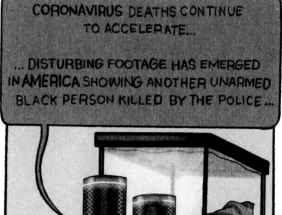

BEN JENNINGS is an award-winning cartoonist for The Guardian, The Economist and others, whose work has exhibited around the world including in London's Cartoon Museum

BELOW: A barn in the middle of a cornfield in rural Ohio, where rural voters supported Trump in record numbers in 2016

Will the centre hold?

Some former supporters say Donald Trump has not delivered on his promise to listen to the USA's forgotten. Will it affect his re-election come November? **Michella Oré** reports

49(03): 68/71 I DOI: 10.1177/0306422020958290

FOUR YEARS AGO, the once "forgotten Americans" emerged centre stage in what would become one of the most contentious presidential elections in the history of the USA. Largely white, lower-middle class and living in a mix of suburban and rural communities, they rallied behind Donald Trump, who pledged not only to listen to their concerns but to make them the driving force behind the country's agenda.

"You will never be ignored again. Your voice, your hopes and your dreams will define our American destiny. And your courage and goodness and love will forever guide us along the way."

Those were some of the many assurances Trump delivered in his inauguration speech. Four years later, do the forgotten Americans feel that they have been listened to?

When Scott Schrock heard Trump's pledge to listen to the citizens who were hard workers and patriots, he was immediately swept up. Schrock, who lives in Ohio, was concerned that the political climate of the country at the time silenced his freedom of speech and prevented true progress from being made. "In the age of political correctness, we needed to be able to speak without being afraid," he told Index.

It wasn't that Schrock completely believed Trump's promise to Make America Great Again, but he appreciated his brash approach to challenging government function which, he felt, was a step in the right direction. "In the age of illogical political jargon and talking points, we needed some common sense," he said. "I resonated with his pro-life stance. I didn't buy all that Trump was selling, but I largely agreed with his view on economics, and it felt good to have someone willing to speak up for us again."

Jessica Freeman, who lives in Georgia, said that while she was disappointed in the lack of a manufacturing resurgence that Trump had promised, she came to accept it as a painful but unfortunate reality.

But it was the Covid-19 pandemic and the country's failure to contain it before more than 170,000 Americans died that caused Freeman to decide she would no longer support Trump. "When the pandemic hit and we needed him to be there to come up with a plan to protect us, he didn't."

Both Schrock and Freeman are members of Republican Voters Against Trump. Comprising "Republicans, former Republicans, conservatives and former Trump voters", the coalition is mobilising against the re-election of Trump this autumn.

For Schrock, the administration's handling of the virus cemented another realisation about Trump's allegiance to the values he ran his 2016 campaign on. He said: "I realised that Trump is not pro-life, as evidenced by his total lack of compassion and focus on the deadly pandemic."

More broadly, the Trump administration's handling of immigration and foreign policy, and the role of the military in state affairs, has created a split in the general solidarity previously shared by his supporters.

For some, Trump is doing exactly what he promised, giving the public a rare glimpse →

I realised that Trump is not pro-life, as evidenced by his total lack of compassion and focus on the deadly pandemic

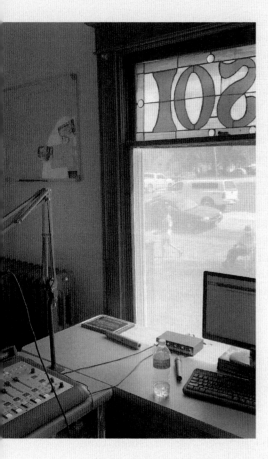

→ into how international relations are conducted, such as in the case of the Ukraine scandal, while challenging the status quo.

"Mr Trump, as crude as he may be and as blind to the defects of his own associates as he is, was nonetheless elected as a force for change," Daniel McCarthy, editor of Modern Age: A Conservative Quarterly, wrote in The New York Times.

But others feel they are still being ignored, with their voices unheard and their wishes unfulfilled. Republican Voters Against Trump has become a home for voters who no longer feel they have one. "Unfortunately, my voice has been lost in this migration to a brand of politics known as Trumpism. I no longer have a political home that represents my values," said Shrock.

Instead of feeling listened to, Schrock feels that the Trump presidency has upended the Republican party which he once felt gave a platform to his voice. Shrock no longer identifies as a Republican.

As to why many voters are still rallying behind Trump and will continue to do so, Freeman believes it comes down to a play on emotions. "He may not have answered your needs, but he's not forgotten how to sway you." ⊗

Michella Oré is a freelance journalist and writer based in New York City, USA

WHO SPEAKS FOR IOWA?

|||||||||||||||||||||||||||||||||||||||||||||||||||||

JAN FOX talks to an Iowa radio station boss about whether Donald Trump's pledge to listen to Middle America was delivered

AT A SMALL community radio station in rural Iowa, owner Joe Hynek is frustrated. Where are the changes that people in his area of Middle America were hoping for when President Donald Trump came to office? It still feels like the farm-belt is not being heard.

"We were hoping for better infrastructure and roads, changes in the 'death tax' to help farmers and continued support for the ethanol industry, which is vital to our state. We got none of it and people are frustrated. The ethanol industry, which was good under the Obama administration, has got worse, not better. Then, corn prices were decent; under Trump, they've tanked."

He added: "I don't see positive change anywhere."

Hynek's station, KSOI, serves his Clarke County town of Murray, population 700, and "neighbouring areas" within a 160-mile radius.

On the station, Hynek's physician sister has a health show; his mum, Angie, deals with funeral announcements; and there's a good mix of community news, a fishing and hunting show, a Bible spot on Sundays and a variety of music programmes. Hynek himself runs the grain report three times a day.

So what are the issues in Murray? He's particularly concerned about things such as the inheritance tax ("death tax") that he says cripples farmers and has led to the disbanding of long-held family farms.

"This administration promised to do something about that, and they've done nothing at all. When you inherit a farm, the tax is so high that it may take years – decades, even – to pay it back. If you inherit a farm worth a million dollars, you're paying $300,000 in taxes. People end up quitting their family farms and it promotes the corporatisation of farms. But our voices on that haven't been heard."

Hynek was also looking for help with more basic improvements for his community. It never came.

"I was hoping we'd get roads – we're really hurting for funds to provide them in rural areas – and we need asbestos water piping replaced with plastic piping. We have drainage issues here in Murray that need funding to do studies so we can improve life here. As a town, we've worked really hard to improve things, but we need help and it's not coming."

One of the worst blows to rural Iowan communities such as Hynek's has been to the ethanol industry. Iowa is the leading ethanol producer in the USA, responsible for almost 30% of the

nation's output. Coronavirus has meant fewer people driving their cars so fuel consumption in general is down, but the Trump administration's policies have delivered a second hit to the industry.

"Forty per cent of all corn grown here in Iowa is used for ethanol production, but Trump played double agent in the push to make ethanol," said Hynek. "There are laws and mandates to include a certain percentage of ethanol in fuel and he started to issue exemptions to the people that mix the fuel, and that really hurt our grain prices."

The administration has also seemingly ignored the effect trade policies would have on the farm-belt communities.

"The trade war with China also meant they stopped buying our soy beans and pork, and that's had a big impact on rural areas like ours."

China is the world's biggest importer of US soy beans but, in a tit-for-tat move, exports slumped when the Trump administration slapped high tariffs on imported Chinese goods.

The market has shown some signs of recovery this year but Iowa farmers may still be lagging behind in revenue.

In Trump's 2016 victory speech, he talked about "the forgotten men and women of our country", declaring that they "will be forgotten no longer", but change has not come to the people of Murray. They still feel as though they lack a voice on the national stage.

One change, though, has come, and Hynek feels it is not a good one. It's a move to further mix religion and politics.

"There's been a push for religion to be included in government. It's fine to be religious, and this is a very faithful area, but America was designed to exclude religion from our governing," he said. "It makes it harder for us all to co-exist as a nation."

Hynek is unsure about how all this will affect the upcoming election, and he still sees a lot of Trump flags flying in his town. Why is this, when it seems as if Iowans' voices haven't been heard?

"It's been very confusing, actually. I don't feel like the people here who voted for Trump really got what they were wanting: the economic lifting, higher paying jobs, keeping more of their tax money," said Hynek.

"Yes, he's been dealing with illegal immigration and rattled the cage with China, which a lot of people seemed to want, but a lot of things he's done have really hurt us.

"But I still hear a lot of support for him in our community. There may be some things that people are not so happy about, but I don't think they are ticked off enough not to vote for him again.

As a town, we've worked really hard to improve things, but we need help and it's not coming

---

I thought we all wanted the same things for America, but maybe not

"They like the idea that someone is protecting their liberties like carrying guns and not wearing facemasks. So they can put up with the other things."

Currently, Hynek has other things on his mind. His wife is a doctor at the local hospital and coronavirus is starting to bite hard in the rural heartland, with numbers taking off after Memorial Day.

In the meantime, Hynek does what he does best: running the station he built himself out of his Victorian home and serving the community. The station stays away from politics, with the closest thing being regular public service announcements encouraging everyone to wear facemasks. It may be contentious for some Trump supporters, but Hynek sees it as a community service.

Their star DJ is a former music store owner who donated his entire record collection to the station when he found out he had to have both his legs amputated due to diabetes.

Since coming on air in 2012, KSOI has remained non-commercial and is supported only by the community. It's small town but not small fry to the people of Murray and its surrounds.

In many rural areas where the internet is still spotty, community radio can be a lifeline and a way for people's voices to be heard. People worry on a daily basis about grain prices and whether they can afford healthcare, hold on to their farms and have decent infrastructure. Hynek worries about all those things, but he also worries about the divisions that the Trump administration has opened up.

"If I had to guess the election, I'd say a lot of people won't go to vote," he said. "I thought we all wanted the same things for America, but maybe not."

Jan Fox is a regular contributor to Index, based in Los Angeles, USA

CULTURE

Past imperfect

Award-winning writer **Lisa Appignanesi** talks lockdown, Twitter and why Vienna inspires her with **Rachael Jolley**

49(03): 74/79 I DOI: 10.1177/0306422020957832

BRITISH-CANADIAN WRITER LISA Appignanesi has found lockdown a difficult time to write, but despite this she has created a new short story exclusively for Index.

Appignanesi, a screenwriter, academic and novelist, said: "It's very hard to move within the instability of the time to something imaginative."

Her story, Lockdown, focuses on an older man, Arthur, who reflects on his past in Vienna during the period between the two world wars.

Appignanesi has a long relationship with the Austrian city.

"I've done an awful lot of work on Viennese literature and, indeed, on Freud, so Vienna always feels very, very close to me and I lived there for a year," she said.

"Vienna is a fascinating place. It was a great city – first of all head of an empire with many, many immigrant groupings in it, and then when it lost its imperial status in World War I it was a very impoverished city."

She says the period of lockdown focused her mind on the restrictions imposed upon the elderly. "I have long thought about what happens to the mind within the body, people's relationship to time in that sense. You grow old and stuff happens to your body and, initially at least, it doesn't seem to affect your mental capacity and the way you grow through time as you are living it."

TOP RIGHT: The author Lisa Appignanesi

She is also interested in the idea of people being present in different ways and how, for instance, the potential anonymity and the disembodied nature of Twitter means that people can unleash their anger differently from how they would if they were in the room with someone.

"Some of the rampant emotions of our time, particularly anger," she said, "were to do with the fact that people on Twitter are not only anonymous but they are disembodied."

In an article for this magazine in 2010, Appignanesi wrote: "The speed of communication the internet permits, its blindness to geography, seems to have stoked the fires of prohibition. The freer and easier it is for ideas to spread, the more punitive the powers that wish to silence or censor become."

Appignanesi, a long-time campaigner for freedom of expression, was born in post-war Poland as Elżbieta Borensztejn. Her Jewish parents had what she has described with understatement as "a difficult war", hiding under different aliases to escape arrest. The family moved then to Paris, which she remembers, and later to Montreal, Canada. She once told BBC Radio 3 that she "grew up with the ghosts of those that died in the concentration camps". Given the family history, it is no wonder she worries about authoritarian governments and restrictions on speech.

She is now concerned about how governments are changing the rules of freedom of expression while the world is distracted by Covid-19, and the threats that may manifest themselves. "Your attention is distracted by something – something happens behind the scenes, and usually the same people are doing the distraction. This time it was the virus."

The freer and easier it is for ideas to spread, the more punitive the powers that wish to silence or censor become

One news item that grabbed her attention recently was about the closure of Guatemala's police archives (see page 27), a library of information about the country's civil war. Her concern is that "those archives are about the disappearances of people under the dictatorships, which were lethal".

As others track governments who want to control the national story, Appignanesi says we must learn from history.

"It's very important for our documents in Britain to be interpreted in different ways, and supplemented by stories we don't know.

"There are always new histories to discover."

ⓧ

Rachael Jolley *is editor-in-chief of Index on Censorship*

Lockdown

Lisa Appignanesi

ARTHUR WAS OLD. Very old. So old that when the word "lockdown" had made its way onto the radio news he was listening to with only half an ear – and even that half tuned to inner voices – he had thought they were talking about him.

It seemed the world was joining him now. In lockdown.

But the whole country had been in metaphorical lockdown for some time, he reflected, its politicians preventing every connection between a fragmented people except angry sparks or empty boasts.

Lockdown was a perfect word to describe his present condition: confined to his cell for his own good by a greater authority. If he promised not to riot, he was allowed out for exercise at regular intervals.

Yet the notion of exercise took all the pleasure out of movement. He preferred to think of it as a walk, better still, a *passeggiata*. He always dressed carefully for the occasion – a suit, perhaps a silk waistcoat, a bow tie. The joy of a stroll was in part that people looked at, and greeted, each other – even smiled. So no stretchy joggers and sweatshirts for him of the kind his grandchildren wore. He liked form. He had always been something of a dandy, though these days, as he heaved what seemed to be boulders rather than legs along the streets, it was harder to turn a casual half smile on the world and appreciate its offerings. But then his senses, too, were in all but lockdown. His new glasses had him stumbling, the ground far closer than where he had last left it, as if he had shrunk back to childhood and well below what was once an adequate height for a man of his generation.

His first grandson had once asked him if he was named after King Arthur since he had a round table and Arthur hadn't liked to contradict him – but the only table that had featured in his own childhood had been the one at the Professor's house in Vienna. He played happily under that

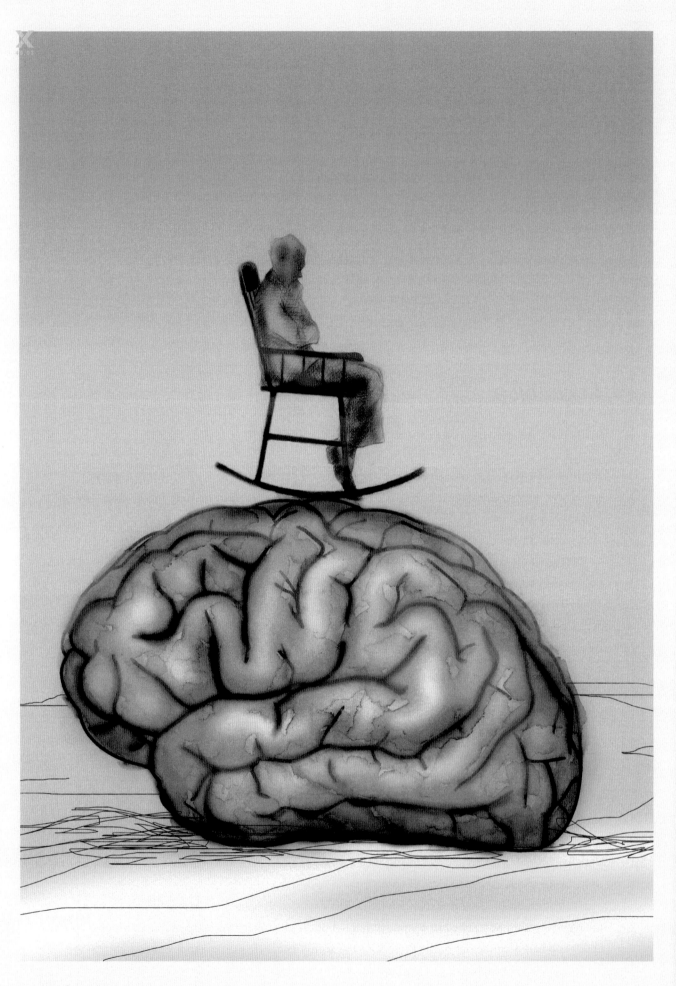

→ while the adults talked and occasionally the Professor would put a hand below the edge of the tablecloth and tousle his hair, then pat him as he did his dogs. He liked the Professor, who gave his name a proper 'T' – Artur. In fact, it was the writer who was called the professor's "*doppelgänger*" who was responsible for Arthur's name.

Doppelgänger was a word he learned early. Another, heard from beneath the table, was *Zensur*. He had thought that had the word hour in it, had thought maybe it meant ten o'clock, *zehn Uhr*. Amidst the chatter of the adult voices, he saw TEN blotting out all the hours that came before, a censoring hour.

Maybe that's why he had this odd relationship to time now, as he reached his midnight. He was convinced that at this late age he finally understood, was indeed living, what Einstein had meant about time slowing in the presence of heavy objects. Arthur was so light now, his bones s0 hollowed out, that time didn't slow for him. It sped.

Or maybe its racing effect was linked to the fact that there was so little of time left that what had once been full and slow was now racing towards an end. The thought of death could no longer be censored or repressed. No bonfire could destroy it. But then it hadn't really worked for

---

Lockdown was a perfect word to describe his present condition: confined to his cell for his own good

---

the books either. They had sprung up in other editions and elsewhere.

Arthur had been born in Berlin just weeks after the great conflagration of books the Nazis had staged and only a few months after the Reichstag fire. His mother had been walking near the Staatsoper on the night of the book burning. She had loved Arthur Schnitzler's work and had known him a little, so he had become little Arthur.

It was as well the Professor was still alive or he might have become Siggy, since his books were in that bonfire too.

Was that why he had spent his life in books and collected so many in the process? He looked up at the study's walls lined in first editions, one side leather bound, the other brighter in their contemporaneity.

"Arthur?"

He checked that the voice was real and forced himself into the present.

In the doorway stood the young woman he liked to think of as his companion, though his granddaughter, Mia, had called her – in insisting on the need for her – an au pair plus. Stella was certainly more than his equal, not only as tall as he once had been but with poise and a razor-sharp intelligence he sometimes thought could penetrate his thoughts without him needing to speak. →

→   So she knew he liked the fact she was decorous and she hadn't – at least not yet – upbraided him for it, as his granddaughter would. Stella was completing a PhD at Cambridge, and with a rueful smile admitted that she had been completing it for an unconscionable while, which most recently had included divorcing her husband. That was why she found herself in need of a room and an extra wage. No one had imagined lockdown.

Now she wanted him up and ready to begin the Sisyphean task of the morning *passeggiata*.

His study door opened onto a terrace and from there down into communal gardens, a square where the trees today were in full glorious flower. He was a lucky man. Doubly lucky that his granddaughter had somehow gifted him this magnificent creature.

"We're going to begin today," Stella said when they paused for him to catch breath beneath the flowering cherry. The sky between its branches was a Mediterranean blue. The blackbirds were in full throat. The young Americans with their twin toddlers weren't out yet.

"I'm not ready." Arthur heard the plaintive high pitch in his own voice and rushed to blur it in a cough.

His cherished memories would be judged through a puritanical lens and turn play into monstrosity

---

"Of course you are! Isn't that what you said when I told you I wasn't ready to write my next chapter."

"Does that mean you have?"

She nodded and took his arm so that the walk could continue.

"But this isn't the same."

"I don't see why not."

He didn't respond. The reasons were too many.

"But it was one of the conditions of my being here, for free, in those wonderful rooms. Mia made that quite clear. Anyhow, I'm interested. I want to do this. We could make a start."

He admired her profile and made an effort to straighten his back. He could imagine how stern she had been over her husband's discovered transgressions.

But now she didn't know what she was asking for. He considered his reluctance once more. Over these last years the project he had set himself, "The Memoirs of Arthur Aske", had foundered irretrievably. Oh there were notes, random paragraphs. But the past was a part-product of the present and the present had changed so quickly, so dramatically, that he could find no focus through which to filter his receding life. This young woman's eye wouldn't help. Never mind his post-war forays into Russia, his work in bringing Zamizdat literature over. Never mind setting up his publishing house or prodding the Austrian government into some recognition of its war-time role. Never mind anything, the loves, the meetings with the greats, the marriages. His cherished memories would be judged through a puritanical lens and turn play into monstrosity. Not that he wanted to narrate the intimate, but censoring himself, trying to step round antics that had felt adventurous and pleasurable in the past, into a current mould felt like tying his memories into a straitjacket. They disintegrated into sawdust in the process. Or maybe that was the flavour of ashes.

The world had had enough of old white, or not quite white, men. Reprobates all. Even his granddaughter – his most loyal prodder – would sit in uncomfortable judgment over him.

"I could ask you questions."

He had missed what she had been saying and only heard this last.

"You could choose not to answer, of course."

"Self-censor, you mean?"

She shrugged. "I hadn't quite meant that, but yes, why not..?" Her look was curious. "There's no such thing as complete honesty about the self, is there?"

"That's what the man under whose table I first heard the word censorship might have said."

She laughed at that, the straitened look leaving her eyes for a moment.

They had made two full circles and the thought came to him that he could happily die this way, meandering round a square on a fine spring day with a companion by his side.

"Come, I'll get some coffee and we can sit on the terrace. Let's begin."

He kept his voice playful, but the look he gave her was direct in its challenge. "Perhaps if there's a story for a story, then? An exchange, I'd like to understand you, too."

She met him on it.

"Let's begin then."

"Women first, surely?"

....

Lisa Appignanesi is an award-winning writer and campaigner for free expression. She is the author of many books including Memory and Desire, Losing the Dead and The Memory Man

The history man

One of China's most widely read writers, **Xue Yiwei**, talks to **Jemimah Steinfeld** about being angry in the 1980s, the importance of history, and his newly translated story

49(03): 80/85 | DOI: 10.1177/0306422020957833

XUE YIWEI WAS just 12 when he had one of the most humiliating experiences of his life. It was the day after China's leader, Mao Zedong, died in 1976 and Xue began to sing a song at home.

Before finishing the first line, however, he realised singing was forbidden during the two-week mourning period and stopped. It was too late. His sister had overheard and reported him to his mother. He was made to kneel in front of a portrait of Mao for two hours.

"I don't think this was an isolated case then, [but] I don't think this would happen in any Chinese family now. Now at home you are free to criticise even the 'Supreme Authority'. Your siblings won't report you and your parents won't punish you. This is a substantial improvement since 1976," said Xue in an interview with Index.

There are echoes of this incident in his short story, which was originally written in Chinese in the late 1980s. This updated English version is published here for the first time.

The story centres on a mythical box of treasures, which supposedly protects a tribe, and its unveiling.

While the story is a parable exploring a broader canvas of humanity, it teems with references to China's past, in particular the transition period from Mao to Deng Xiaoping, who ushered in a new era for China in which one phrase became infamous: "Let some people get rich first".

Xue reflects on this, saying: "In 1979, when this slogan first struck our ears, some were confused, some were laughing, while some were excited."

He says the first decade of reform and opening up was a time "full of idealism", which most Chinese intellectuals considered "a golden time". But it was short-lived.

By the time Xue penned the story, he describes himself as an "an angry young man".

"It was a hard time for the Chinese intellectuals when 'bourgeois liberalisation' became the main target of censorship," he said. Then came Tiananmen.

"The year 1989 was certainly a watershed," said Xue, in reference to the protests and subsequent massacre.

Xue, who took part in the protests in Changsha, a city in China's south, wrote about the aftermath in a novella called December 31, 1989. The reaction to the publication was intense – the magazine which published it was threatened with closure and Xue had to stop writing for five years. Eventually, in 2002, he moved to Canada.

"Free speech is the life of literature," he said, adding that part of his reason for moving was to gain more independence as a writer. The move bore fruit – he has published more than 20 books since 2012 and many of them are critically acclaimed.

Xue is one of the most widely read authors in China today, with his work frequently making Asian top 10 lists, yet some of his highest profile books have not been published there. Dr Bethune's Children, for example, was turned down by editors because it allegedly "harmed"

RIGHT: Chinese writer Xue Yiwei, who moved to Canada following years of being punished for what he wrote

He was made to kneel in front of a portrait of Mao for two hours

China's reputation. That most of his writing has reached so many in China is in large part due to individuals who have taken their own risks along the way.

"The amazing thing about China is that it is such a big country you could always find a courageous and supportive person to make something happen for literature," he said, adding that one day he intends to write a book about these people: the editors, the publishers, even the officials in charge of cultural affairs.

Xue believes the challenges writers face today are different to those when he left. The space for young writers has shrunk "dramatically" – in part because of finances. It is simply too expensive to be a full-time writer for most in China today.

"Literature is no longer a glorious career," he said.

And Xue, who has lived through some of the biggest historical moments in China's recent past, and seen how it can be manipulated, believes "history is becoming a 'forbidden city'

The amazing thing about China is that it is such a big country you could always find a courageous and supportive person to make something happen for literature

that literature could not, and should not, visit".

"But how could literature be isolated from history?" he asked. "Without history, literature is lame, is sick, is only a skeleton of empty words." ⊗

Jemimah Steinfeld *is the deputy editor of* Index on Censorship *magazine*

Treasured box

by Yiwei Xue

GRANDFATHER DOES NOT have long to live. Were his illness not so severe, we would still have to go to his room every night to sit before him and listen to the same story he has told us countless times. It was a ritual from which no one could be absent, even Shorty, Grandfather's favourite. One night, Shorty sneaked out to the hill to watch the phosphorescent light that rises from the bodies of the dead. By the time he came back, shaking with fear, Grandfather had just finished telling the story. We assumed Shorty's first offence would be treated with leniency, but after fixing his favourite grandchild with an unyielding gaze, Grandfather announced his punishment: Shorty would spend the whole night kneeling before the portrait of our greatest ancestor, forbidden to sleep.

There were details in the story that never failed to captivate us, no matter how many times we heard them. Chief among these was the appearance of the enemy. Grandfather's descriptions were so bizarre that we were simply unable to picture what they must have looked like.

→   Then there was the end of the story, our inexorable victory! Our triumph was not a result of wits, or of luck, but the protection afforded to us by the treasures we had safely sealed in an iron box. It is said that these treasures have been with us for generations, the greatest inventions of our greatest ancestor, created at a time when our enemies were still savages to whom even the meaning of the word "invention" was unknown.

"With the iron box intact, we are indomitable." This is how Grandfather would end the story each night.

Every evening we heard how the enemy burned our homes to the ground, one after the other. They plundered all our silver, destroyed all our books and defiled all our women – yet despite this, our tribe had not disappeared from the Earth.

Many years later we had rebuilt our houses, produced more silver, taught a new generation of scholars and scribes, and our women had given birth to many more children. The story concluded with a message of hope and of light.

Once Grandfather had finished telling the story we had to ask questions. It was a time when Grandfather encouraged us to speak freely, to ask whatever was on our minds, to fear not for any offence it may cause.

"Grandfather, why didn't the enemy steal the iron box?"

"They did not know that it existed," Grandfather would say. "And even if they had they would not have known where it was hidden, just as you do not know today."

"Grandfather, if the enemy had stolen the iron box would they have become indomitable too?"

"The treasures are bound by principles of virtue," Grandfather would reply. "They offer protection to us only."

"Grandfather, how much silver did they plunder?"

"Grandfather, were the new scholars and scribes able to rewrite the books that were destroyed?"

"Grandfather, what does 'defile' mean? Why did the enemy want to defile our women?"

"Grandfather, why are the enemy's weapons always more powerful than ours?"

"Grandfather, were there good people among the enemy? As good as or better than us?"

"Grandfather, why did the enemy look so strange? How could their eyes have been blue?"

"Grandfather, if their eyes were blue what colour were their tears?"

"Grandfather, why can the enemy never get along with us? Why do they always have to invade our territory?"

And so it would continue, until someone asked the inevitable question.

"Grandfather, what exactly is in the iron box?"

This was the question Grandfather liked least. After a long period of silence, he would say: "Treasures. Priceless treasures," in a voice so quiet he did not seem to be speaking to us.

"What kind of treasures? Could you describe them for us?"

Grandfather would lower his head sorrowfully. He had never seen the treasures in the iron   →

→ box. The story he had told us countless times was a story he in turn had heard as a child every evening in his grandfather's room. Back then, when the same question was asked, his grandfather, too, would lower his head.

"Grandfather, you really don't know what the treasures look like?"

Grandfather would lift his head with the same pained look in his eyes. "No, I do not know," he would say, his voice full of regret, just like his grandfather before him.

Shorty always appeared to be engrossed in the story, but unlike everyone else he never asked any questions. When the story was over, he would lift his head and stare dumbly at the spider webs in the rafters, and Grandfather never pressed him to join in with the questioning.

From the moment Shorty was born it was clear he was different. He had a strange way of looking at things, and when he spoke, we found it difficult to follow what he was trying to say. Whenever he opened his mouth it was hard for us not to laugh.

Grandfather does not have long to live so we no longer have to go to his room every evening. When the sun sets, some of us go to the fields to catch loaches and frogs while others lie by the barn

---

Three days after the funeral, a witchdoctor identifies the contents of the iron box as the skeletons of a fish, a rat, a frog and a bird

---

to crack jokes and count stars. Shorty goes night after night to the graveyard to watch the phosphorescent streaks that emanate there, drawn to them as though they contained some inexhaustible mystery. We all appear to have completely forgotten about the iron box and the sealed treasures.

Grandfather, on the other hand, cannot stop thinking about them. A thought has occurred to him and won't leave him be. He wants to break the rules of the tribe. Before he dies, he wants to open the box and see the treasures inside. Uncle Xianfu, whose name literally means "get rich first" and who stands guard day and night by Grandfather's side, supports this idea: "You hold the position of Supreme Authority in the tribe. Who would dare deny your right to know the truth?"

Eventually, one day, under the pressure of Uncle Xianfu's exhortations, Grandfather nods his head.

A great ceremony is quickly arranged. On the final day of the month of fasting, Uncle Xianfu helps Grandfather out of his sickbed and leads him to the chair that symbolises his Supreme Authority and in which he once sat every night to tell us the story. Our chairs are arranged around it according to the rules of our tribe. No one pays any attention to Shorty's empty chair.

After solemnly explaining that the opening of the iron box is not a matter of satisfying a personal desire but is in accordance with the Will of the Heavens, Grandfather raises his hand to signal to Uncle Xianfu that the time has come to enact Providence. Uncle Xianfu looks loftily around him before striding portentously out of the room.

Enough time passes that we are getting restless when we hear the sound of cursing from outside. Uncle Xianfu bursts in with Shorty's ear pinched between the fingers of his left hand and the iron box held in his right. "The kid knew where the box was. He got there before I could."

Uncle Xianfu's voice is quivering with anger. He lets go of Shorty, opens the iron box, the seal now broken, and places it before Grandfather.

Grandfather leans forward slightly and peers into the box. A look of disgust appears on his face before he closes his eyes and turns his head to one side.

It takes some time before Grandfather is able to regain his composure. He turns his compassionate gaze to Shorty, who is visibly trembling. "Where are the treasures?" he asks persuasively. "Those treasures belong to the whole tribe." All that can be seen in the iron box are four small skeletons.

"That's all there was! That's all there was!" Shorty protests. "Those are the treasures that have been protecting us!"

As always when Shorty speaks, we find ourselves bursting into laughter, but then Grandfather appears to choke on something. His body spasms and he keels over.

Not much care is taken with the funeral because no one can muster the energy. Except for Shorty and Uncle Xianfu, no one thinks there remains any hope for the tribe.

Three days after the funeral, a witchdoctor identifies the contents of the iron box as the skeletons of a fish, a rat, a frog and a bird. A great many discussions follow on the subject of whether the treasures are still worth keeping.

Shorty has become much more talkative and is an active participant in these debates. He argues passionately that we must continue to protect the iron box, for its contents are not simply treasures left to us by our ancestors, but what will ensure the future of the tribe.

We suspect that his insistence is a result of his deep respect for Grandfather and his profound guilt for what happened, even if he attempts to console us by saying that Grandfather died a perfectly natural death. There is nothing to be melancholy about, Shorty claims, and even less to justify losing hope.

We have a great deal to be getting on with. "Look forward," he says, this is the proper attitude to have. It is for this reason that Shorty advocates a "rejuvenation" of the Supreme Authority and supports Uncle Xianfu for the role. Only Uncle Xianfu, he claims, can lead the tribe onto a new path, a path to prosperity and strength. This, he says, is the most important revelation he received from the phosphorescent light of history that appears at night over the graves of the dead.

---

*Translated by **Stephen Nashef***

*Xue Yiwei** is the author of many books including Dr Bethune's Children and Shenzheners. His latest book, King Lear and Nineteen Seventy-Nine (2020) is currently being translated into English*

Four more years?

Mark Frary sets out the key issues ahead of the US election, setting the context for **Kaya Genç**'s surreal short story looking at the election from a dog's eye view

49(03): 86/91 I DOI: 10.1177/0306422020957834

Not so long ago, someone started chanting "Four more years". It quickly echoed across the USA, and Obama was duly re-elected. Now, in the run-up to the 2020 election in November, that same mantra is running round the electorate's heads. For President Donald Trump's supporters, it will be an earnest call for more of the same. His opponents worry it could lead to four more years of eroding basic freedoms.

Recent polls show the Democrats in the ascendancy, and Joe Biden's choice of Kamala Harris as his vice-presidential running mate may push their approval ratings higher still. It is making Trump nervous and he has already started grumbling about the freedom to vote by mail.

Many of the rights enshrined in the constitution have come under attack under Trump. The heavy-handed response of the police to largely peaceful protests after the murder of George Floyd brought into question whether Trump believes in the freedom of assembly.

Trump has shown his feelings for Islam over a long period – questioning whether his predecessor was Muslim, suggesting he would consider closing mosques and, in 2017, issuing an executive order that largely targeted Muslims.

So much for freedom of religious belief.

But it is the freedom of the press that is perhaps most at risk. US Press Freedom Tracker has reported more than 650 attacks on the press during the Black Lives Matters protests. Some say Trump's own track record in undermining journalists has cultivated an environment in which people can threaten the media with impunity.

Trump showed in 2016 that he doesn't necessarily need the traditional press to win, but he will have a harder time in 2020 thanks to his bungled response to Covid-19.

The election is going to be juicy for the media to cover. With Harris on the Democratic ticket, LGBTQ and women's rights and justice are going to be key issues.

But Harris is hot on media freedom, too, and there is likely to be a clear divide between the two campaigns over that. In 2017, Trump tweeted a Gif of a lookalike at a wrestling match flooring someone whose head had been replaced with a CNN logo. The tweet was "liked" half a million times. In response, Harris calmly tweeted: "The First Amendment [of the constitution] and freedom of the press are critical to our democracy. The latest attack from the [White House] undermines our values."

It highlighted the different approaches by the two politicians to the First Amendment. One considers the freedom of the press to be a challenge to his manhood while the other sees it as a core freedom that helps the USA to flourish.

If his figures get worse, Trump's media attacks will increase as he blames everyone but himself. It will be a sad day for democracy if it gives his supporters free rein to do the same. ⊗

Mark Frary is associate editor of Index

One considers the freedom of the press to be a challenge to his manhood while the other sees it as a core freedom

The Duty

by Kaya Genç

I'M DONALD TRUMP'S dog. I speak three languages. I have a mahogany coat with black markings. My tongue is warm and wet. My black muzzle and erect ears mislead some to believe that my name is German Shepherd. It is not. Neither am I called Rudy Giuliani, Katie Hopkins or Nigel Farage. Call me Fido. Plain and simple.

I'm a mongrel. I'm in between breeds and existences. I've been here a long time. I know how the White House operates. I know where to poo and where to pee-pee. I know where Donald Trump keeps his tax returns (38.8977° N, 77.0365° W, in a tin box labelled 'PANDORA'S BOX').

My best friend's name is Dale. He's the head groundskeeper. He's the one who delivered me to Donald Trump. Dale can see ghosts and converse with our lot. I've haunted him for months in the White House garden before he invited me back to life.

At the White House, most days begin with Dale. We leave early in the morning to inspect plants. Under his watch I wander among fragrant magnolias, green boxwoods, upright tulips and crab apple blossoms. Our garden is a National Park. I feel awful after pooping behind bushes, fearing staining our history. But history is a subject my master ignores. His face was blank when Dale introduced me to him as "Fido". I thought every American knew who Fido was. But Donald Trump didn't know about Abraham Lincoln's mongrel dog. When I looked to him for a sign of recognition his eyes were hollow.

This morning, Dale talked about Bo and Sunny, "Obama's dogs". They didn't poo much, he claimed.

"They can poo and be cool at the same time," I said. "Don't worry."

Dale gets real emotional when he pronounces the word Obama. "Obama's Portuguese water dogs had their own media schedules," he said, his eyes watering, his upper lip trembling.

I wish I had got to know them – Bo had a white chest while Sunny, in Dale's description, was "all-black". But black is a colour Donald Trump doesn't savour.

For my old master, shot in the head by an actor in a Washington theatre, black lives mattered. He's long gone and buried but Old Abe will live in my heart forever. He was thoughtful and diplomatic; kind, skillful, benevolent. I loved Honest Abe's sons, Tad and Willie, like my own. I carried parcels for them, rooting for the success of the Republican Party. But politics abounded with two things I couldn't stand – pomposity and noise. It still does.

After Dale unleashed me, I climbed the stairs to the second floor and jumped into the Lincoln Bedroom to search for my master. He wasn't there. I headed to the Queen's Bedroom, sniffing carpets and peeking into the Yellow Oval Room. He wasn't there either.

I found him sitting, Buddha-like, on the presidential bed in his bedroom. He radiated an orange light, smelled like gum, and produced a batch of incomprehensible sounds.

→   "Traitor," his curled lips were saying when I entered. "Dog! Foulmouthed lowlife." His tongue danced on his pursed lips for a moment; his eyebrows flickered with each message he read. Hunchbacked and fully dressed he fondled a tablet to inspect the latest on the November election.

News, insistently negative, upset him. "Sleepy Joe" led by 10 percentage points. "Quid Pro Joe" had an 11-percent lead. "Sleepy Creepy" had a 12-percentage-point margin. "Wacko John Bolton" became a New York Times bestseller with his Tell-All. I wanted to raise my poor master's spirits, so I jumped to his feet and was set to lick him.

People say Donald Trump is a "germaphobe". My experience is different. While his tiny hand patted my soft head, I mouthed his free hand. I licked his fingers first, delighting in his gnawed fingernails and wet knuckles, while the other fingers rested on my skull. My new master isn't a great caresser. He doesn't much care for hygiene either. He used the hand I licked to pick his nose later, while the other – unlicked – hand tap-tap-tapped the glossy tablet.

Donald Trump is an early-bird who enjoys taking long-bullshits first thing in the morning, so I wasn't surprised. As he composed his messages, I crouched next to him and closed my eyes, imagining my curly hair entering Donald Trump's body, seeds of geraniums and canna lilies circulating in his system and blossoming in his lungs.

Such experiences move me as a highly impressionable dog. This must be why my old master's spectre abruptly materialised in front of me a minute later. After he was gunned down I'd mourned Old Abe for months before I, too, was murdered by a violent man who couldn't stand kind souls. Now the Great Emancipator's spectre eyed me warmly, but his wise face expressed such disdain for the man whose hand I'd been licking that I inadvertently bit it on the wrist. The tablet dropped; the orange man got up to his feet, exposed and terrified. He kicked me in the stomach twice before exiting the bedroom.

There is no justice on this earth: bigots prevail; anti-Semites and kneelers-on-black-bodies flourish; resentment wins the day. I'll avenge Wise Abe's death and those heinous kicks.

*   *   *

I've been Donald Trump's dog for a month now. I don't recommend it, unless you wear a Make America Great Again hat. It was Jared and Ivanka who advised Donald Trump to get a dog, back in August. Jared claimed it would look good politically. I'd accompany his father-in-law while he took shelter from the "Kung Flu". There'd be publicity pics on social media to persuade elderly white Democrats into changing their votes. That was the plan.

When Dale brought me in, the Kushners cheered. But after the biting incident, my master began to strike a different chord. He couldn't handle his iPhone or Coke can the way he used to. "I don't know," he mumbled as Ivanka, a real lady, sliced her peppered steak in the Dining Room this afternoon. "I don't feel good with this dog. He feels a little phoney to me."

"I've been no enemy of dogs, Princess," he continued, eyeing the sliced meat with disdain.

"Chappy, Ivana's poodle, you remember him, you know we used to sleep and lick cones together. Then Chappy and I had this fight over the chinchilla coat – remember that, Princess? Chappy didn't want me near Ivana's closet, fearing I'd steal the chinchilla coat. But I didn't steal the chinchilla coat. I don't steal chinchilla coats, Princess. Honestly, I don't steal!"

He closed his eyes like a meditating Sufi.

"Then Ivana said, 'It's me and Chappy, or no one,' and I knew I couldn't stand 'no one' and →

→ would prefer 'anyone' and so Chappy stayed but he continued to bark at me territorially."

He added: "I should've fired him like a dog."

Ivanka looked completely nonplussed. I followed her slim legs as they exited the Dining Room and walked downstairs to the ground floor. She seemed a little shaken; her father might soon be voted out of office "like a dog" (his words). I feared they'd put me to sleep "for reciprocity" (his words).

But Ivanka is a kind soul. I followed her as she entered the White House Library. We waited silently, like two virgins in a nunnery. The room was small – just seven square metres. I could feel Ivanka's frustration and sadness. To console her, I crouched next to her high-heeled shoes.

Back in the 19th century, Old Abe used this room for laundry. I can still smell the perfume of his trousers. In Dale's telling, Abigail Fillmore later established a White House Library, which Herbert Hoover transported down here. Hoover, too, was a true Republican. As a conservative dog I miss his breed.

It was three o'clock when Donald Trump joined his daughter and placed his big bum on a mahogany chair by the fireplace. He was facing a lighthouse clock, and I saw the portrait of George Washington eyeing us from above. Much to my surprise, Washington began to wink and spoke in

---

Chappy didn't want me near Ivana's closet, fearing I'd steal the chinchilla coat. But I didn't steal the chinchilla coat. I don't steal chinchilla coats, Princess. Honestly, I don't steal!

---

a husky voice that only I could hear. "What's up, Fido?" he said. "You all right in there, doggy? Careful with that orange man. I have one thing to ask from you, Fido, and that is to save the Republic from the orange man. But no pressure. Just find a media-hand-grenade for the November election. Do it, Fido! It's your duty."

He signed off mysteriously: "Old Abe sends his warm regards."

Not knowing what to do I offered my head to Ivanka. She placed a kiss on it, but her father seemed beyond consoling. His phone, buzzing with likes and retweets, was his life's sole joy. To give them space I began inspecting book jackets and additions to the collection – works by George Saunders, Toni Morrison and The Heart of a Dog by the Russian writer Bulgakov caught my eye. I also found a volume titled Think Big and Kick Ass, penned by my master.

Just then a roaring sound came from the direction of the fireplace: "BOLTON! That dog!" It was as if a thunder bolt had struck Ivanka's head; she started running around in panic, her hands raised to the sky, asking gods for a divine intervention. They didn't.

"Nothing escapes my GAZE," the orange man roared as he threw that book, authored by a true Republican, into orange flames. I watched it burn to ashes.

Only after that did my master's attention shift to "Fox and Friends". To boost his pleasure, he tried opening a can of Coke. "My wrist hurts like hell!" he screamed. "I'll fire you like a dog! Princess, please open this for me." Ivanka complied as her father, like a bored child, watched colourful images morphing into each other. Ivanka, a damsel in distress, seemed so sad that I wanted to lick her cheeks to raise her spirits. She said Jared would organise a press briefing the following morning. "You could perform one of your tricks," she said, as if Donald Trump was a circus dog.

I decided to spend the night in the garden. But I couldn't sleep. I hallucinated the Great Emancipator guiding me inside the White House to find secret documents while I took short breaks to lick my butt. "Exit the Library, open the fourth door on your left," said the Ancient One. Around 6am I entered Dale's room and licked his neck and eyebrows and he promised to place me next to the president during the presser. We were ready.

"Someone from CNN? I love CNN. Objective and unpopular," my master said, in answer to a well-dressed man's question.

"Just pass the microphone to the Bruce Lee on the front row. He's Xi's man, look how well-behaved he is. That's how journalists act under dictatorships. Take note!" Still, the CNN reporter refused to hand back the microphone.

"Don't push my hand here, just don't push it," my boss said, his right wrist visibly in pain. "Or I'll have to kick you out like a dog. You don't like that, do you? I'm a bit harsher than Lincoln. I'm tougher than Obama. Now leave the room please."

While "Bruce Lee" began formulating a question I ran after the CNN reporter and threw the wet, much licked ball I'd concealed in my mouth on his Hush Puppies. He thought I was throwing up; on closer inspection the reporter noticed what I'd handed to him – a handwritten note by Dale. It read: "For Access to Orange Man's Tax Returns, Follow Fido."

Aided by Dale and a Secret Service agent I dare not name (his name begins with S!) we sneaked onto the ground floor and made our way to the Map Room. The reporter, delirious for the scoop he'd been handed in the form of warm vomit, fainted. I had to paw his crotch to wake him up. Once reactivated he took the tin box and jumped out of the window and ran so fast he disappeared from our sight in less than 33 seconds.

The next morning, I strolled in our National Park and wandered among crab apple blossoms and green boxwoods when a newsboy threw the latest issue of the Washington Post in the bushes where I relieved my bladder each morning. There it was: the Tax Return headline, the portrait of a frustrated president, and the predicted landslide of "Very Slow Sleepy" on 3 November. For a moment I wanted to pee-pee and poo on that historic front page but decided against it. I'm Donald Trump's dog. I'm a mongrel loyal to two masters. Some think they can fire me like a dog; and as a dog I can fire a master if I feel like it. I mouthed the newspaper, gave it a good lick and headed to the orange man's bedroom.

Kaya Genç is a novelist and essayist from Istanbul. He is contributing editor at Index for Turkey

Speech patterns

Abraham T Zere tells **Orna Herr** about escaping one of the world's most censored countries, Eritrea, to find himself living in Trump's USA

49(03): 92/96 I DOI: 10.1177/0306422020957836

January 2012, I was walking on a tightrope," Zere said, adding that he could have been "arrested any time, by anyone".

He has since been granted political asylum in the USA and it is from there that he speaks to Index about his short story, The Speech, which is published here in English for the first time.

He describes it as "an experimental story" and one that "does not read as a fictional work in the Eritrean setting".

The opening scene introduces the reader to 12 men who are about to travel to China for training and Beraki Bockretsion, the chief of the biometrics unit at the police station where the men are gathered.

"I was inspired by Eritrean political elites' empty rhetorical speeches. Although I took that as inspiration, I have tried to convey a universal message; reducing power to its rightful place – emptiness," said Zere.

"I was trying to show the clichéd speeches… that trickle down from the country's top leader to the smallest unit leader or least relevant bureaucrat. In most authoritarian regimes, everyone tries to mimic the top leadership and they adopt their words and styles."

Bockretsion's speech alludes to the men having been cherry-picked to take part in the training.

Zere explains that this kind of language is exploited to inspire ill-placed loyalty to the regime, saying: "It is such ego-feeding, where each part feeds upon their delusions. That is also how dictatorship sustains, in a way."

Eritrea is a one-party state ruled by long-running president Isaias Afwerki, and is known as one of the world's most secretive countries.

Does this impact on Zere, even in exile?

"Many of us who either follow events from

ERITREAN WRITER ABRAHAM T Zere fled his home country in 2012 in search of safety in the USA. But since he arrived, the political landscape and attitudes towards the press and immigrants have become almost unrecognisable under President Donald Trump.

For Zere, this is a source of personal concern.

"As a black person whose country is now under a [US-imposed] travel ban and, more importantly, who is living under political asylum, I have lots of anxieties," he said in an interview with Index.

Although Zere travelled in and out of the USA several times in recent years, he was always worried that he could be questioned at US customs as he has criticised Trump in the public domain.

"Although this did not happen, subconsciously I prepared to defend myself if I were to be asked about what I wrote," he said.

"This is a prelude to self-censorship. This might force someone in my position to think what they write as it might affect their future."

Zere fled Eritrea after information minister Ali Abdu published a public arrest warrant notice for him in 2009, labelling him a national security threat.

"All this time, until I left the country in

Until I left the country in January 2012, I was walking on a tightrope

afar, or have experienced it first-hand, are living in a permanent nervous state. Many Eritrean journalists are rotting in underground prisons, the majority since 2001... My concern as a citizen who is associated with media and literature is doubled.

"I have been watching steadily as many of my colleagues, associates and mentors end up in dungeons, never to be charged or heard of since." ⊗

Orna Herr *is editorial assistant at Index*

The Speech

Abraham T Zere

AS WE WERE preparing for a six-month course to be offered in China, 12 of us – representing five ministries and other government institutes – were sent to the central police station for biometric testing as part of the procedure for obtaining passports. As we had no reason to rush after providing the fingerprints (results were to be collected the next day), we waited for one another outside the office, chattering excitedly.

After a short time passed, a woman, possibly an assistant, came out and said that her boss was waiting inside and invited us to come in. A man dressed in a faded brand-name suit, red tie and equally faded blue shirt – indisputably the boss – shook our hands in turn. He directed us to the eight available seats.

With some of our dozen having to share seats, we made ourselves as comfortable as possible. The man watched us as we settled in and then finally broke the silence. "I know you are in a hurry and I will try to shorten it. I have brief remarks that I want to share with you about your travel."

He scanned us slowly with his eyes to make sure we were ready and attentive.

"All right, how was your day so far?"

(Uncoordinated but loud sounds of gratitude.)

He continued: "I feel honoured to introduce myself to you. I am Beraki Bockretsion, the chief of the biometrics unit."

(Absolute silence.)

"Yemane has informed me yesterday that you are coming to do the fingerprints. I have been waiting for you as I have a short note of advice."

With each sentence, Bockretsion's voice got louder, stronger and more commanding. It didn't take me long to recognise that he was a master of such meetings.

Quietly we listened. He sipped water from his glass, adjusted his seat, then took out papers and started reading in a loud and commanding tone.

→   *   *   *

LADIES AND GENTLEMEN, honorary travellers!

(I looked around quickly and all of us were men. Absolute silence.)

On behalf of my office and, by extension, the Eritrean government, I greet and congratulate you on such historic accomplishments in your lives. It is in difficult circumstances that you are preparing to take a huge national responsibility, which is a big step in achieving your ultimate dreams. I can't stress enough the honour and privilege I am bestowed with to stand in front of you at this podium to share my short, yet imperative nationalistic guidance.

Dear ladies and gentlemen!

I doubt any one of you here is unaware of the economic hardships and abject poverty our nation has suffered from during its long history of colonial rule. After the country's independence, to rehabilitate the devastated economy we inherited, to catch up on the lost years and achieve equality with other nations, we started from scratch and toiled hard to stand on our feet. One of the significant markers and bold initiatives taken after the country's independence was the Eritrean government's firm commitment to enhance its educational sector. The Eritrean people and their government have invested everything in your education. This, of course, is with the hope and strong belief that you will, one day, pay back your government. The initiative doesn't stop there. As a continuation of Eritrea's principled stand and unwavering sustenance, now we are preparing you for higher education.

The six-month-long course will combine theoretical and practical training. Distinguishing this scholarship is the fact that it's being offered at a critical time when the nation is facing existential internal and external plots and threats. No matter the severity of these threats, I am confident that they will be challenged and overcome as they always have before. You are preparing to take a big mission, and I call upon you to be worthy of this mission!

This is not the first time the Motherland is firmly confronting and withstanding perfidious attacks by foreign enemies. World history has well documented that before the strategic withdrawal of 1978, the Eritrean Liberation Front heroically fought to dismantle the enemy. Despite world powers siding with our enemies, the brave Front fully encircled the capital until it was reassigned for tactical manoeuvres.

Since then, the Motherland has steadfastly marched ahead against all odds and unremitting hostilities from all directions. With every antagonistic attack, Eritreans add another shield of resoluteness. Let's leave it to history to document and judge who will come out victorious.

At times couched as border disputes, other times through their minions, the repeated tricks

of the bigger powers and their interventions have been foiled thanks to the farsighted Eritrean government, the unwavering support of our defence forces, and the unyielding citizens who always side with our prudent leadership. These attacks will always be defied and forever challenged.

Ladies and gentlemen!

From the early days of independence, the Eritrean government has enacted crystal-clear policies. They are based on the principle of collaboration, mutual understanding, and empowering →

→ the youth. This model has its roots in the long patriotic history of the nation. That is why the government has selected the brightest future leaders of the nation from different ministries and is now sending you to China for special training.

Without the need to prepare for the future, I do not think many of you would miss the fact that ex-freedom fighters who have commanded crucial battles during the war of independence are better deserving than you of such an honoured opportunity. However, the cornerstone of the Eritrean government's upright position is unambiguous: It has been to strive hard to achieve our long-term plans by training the rising generation.

The government is investing every penny in you, hoping for far better outcomes. We are cognisant of the fact that some of our citizens will fall short of our noble expectations and deviate from their mission. However, we expect all of you to return to the most blessed nation right after completing your education. Once you are back from your training, you will be entrusted with repairing the deteriorating infrastructure our nation has inherited from the colonial forces.

I doubt any of you need a reminder from me, but you are expected to work hard and shoulder the responsibility in achieving the bigger dream. As we expect great contributions from you, I believe and hence call upon you to excel at your endeavours.

Wherever they have been sent for higher studies, as witnessed with older generations of Eritrean students in Cairo and Russia, Eritreans have consistently excelled among their peers. I am full of confidence you are preparing to repeat history and attain similar crowning achievements. Let their history inspire you! I call on you to work hard – not only to overtake cohorts in your courses, but to even outstrip the records held in the school by previous students and take your success to a global level. This is not only my opinion but the conviction of the Eritrean government at large.

Ladies and gentlemen!

In the increasingly interconnected and fast-paced age of globalisation, where the world is turning into one big village, I trust that you will make use of the modern technological tools and fast-changing internet communications in order to catch up, and excel with rapid developments in the competitive world without opening a crack among your group, helping each other, strengthening your companionship and love, where you will solve any rifts among yourselves amicably and in a civilised way, I call upon you to stand together and face the challenges.

Eternal glory to our martyrs who made us see this light!

Victory to the masses!!

Beraki Bockretsion

Unit head, biometrics office – Asmara

....

Abraham T Zere is a US-based Eritrean exiled writer and journalist. This story was first published in Tigrinya in his book ኣል አ ዘዮቱ (Nothing Else Emkulu, 2020) and is published in English here for the first time, translated by himself

New tactics to close down speech

Orna Herr reports on how laws are increasingly being used against journalists

49(03): 97/100 I DOI: 10.1177/0306422020958292

RIGHT: Rappler news editor Miriam Grace Go (left) with investigative editor Chay Hofileña in the Rappler newsroom

BELOW: Filipino President Rodrigo Duterte. Duterte has carried out a sustained attack on Rappler, a Manila-based news outlet

"**THAT'S THE FIRST** step in attacking press freedom ... they attack your credibility and when they've succeeded in destroying your credibility in front of ordinary people, it's easy for the government to supplement that with propaganda," Miriam Grace Go, the news editor at Manila-based news website Rappler, told Index about the tactics used by Filipino President Rodrigo Duterte and his government.

In a move to defend freedom of speech against Duterte's attacks, Index became one of 78 civil society and journalist organisations which comprise the #HoldTheLine Coalition. The coalition demanded that the authorities in the Philippines dropped trumped-up tax evasion charges against Rappler and its founder, Maria Ressa. Ressa appeared in court on 22 July and pleaded not guilty.

At the time of writing, she is waiting on the judge's decision. If found guilty, Ressa could be sentenced to 44 years behind bars.

In another attack on Rappler, Ressa was found guilty of cyber-libel on 15 June and could face six years in prison. She is currently on bail.

Speaking in the wake of Ressa's court appearance, Go said: "The attacks have been about casting doubts

on the credibility of the news organisation – having gender-based attacks on our reporters, things like that. We knew it could worsen over time, so when they filed the cyber-libel charge against Maria, although it was filed by a businessman, we knew that the businessman had connections to the government and it came with other cases filed by the government."

Asked if the attacks had caused a chilling effect in the Rappler newsroom, Go said "we were prepared for this battle", but added that there could be a ripple effect. "The smaller news operations would think that if the government can do this to Maria and to Rappler, who have international support, then they can easily do that to smaller newsrooms."

Speaking about the tax charges, Go said that, ironically, Rappler has been acknowledged as a high corporate taxpayer by the city where the court trying them is based.

"You can see the irony, you can see the contradiction, but you will also see that this government will do what it wants to do to intimidate media organisations," she said.

The use of legal channels to attempt to silence journalists is also an issue in Europe. Jessica Ní Mhainín, senior policy research →

> *You will also see that this government will do what it wants to do to intimidate media organisations*

BELOW: Maria Ressa, founder of Philippines news organisation Rappler. Ressa is facing trumped-up tax charges which could see her behind bars for 44 years.

→ and advocacy officer at Index, has authored a second report on strategic lawsuits against public participation (Slapps), which will be published this month (see the preview in this issue on page 66). The report is based on discussions at an Index-organised roundtable of some of the top lawyers on this issue from Europe and the USA, and their recommendations for taking action to stop lawsuits being used in this way.

Ní Mhainín says action is needed across Europe to stop this attack on the freedom of the media.

"Even in the media, some are unaware that the law is being used to intimidate and silence critical voices," she said. "Most people have heard about growing inequality, but few realise the extent to which some wealthy and powerful entities are using their vast means to restrict access to certain information or curtail their freedom of speech."

To highlight global attacks on press freedom, Index has launched Index Shots, a series of video interviews on freedom of expression issues.

In one of the first in the series, editor-in-chief Rachael Jolley interviewed Özlem Dalkıran, a Turkish human rights activist and a member of the Citizen's Assembly, who was arrested in 2017 during a workshop about social media and digital security.

On 3 July, Dalkıran was sentenced to 25 months in prison on charges of aiding terrorism. She had been arrested with nine other activists.

Dalkıran said: "It was a shocking experience because we were not arrested through a demonstration ... or for something that you actually did as part of your job."

When Jolley asked what impact the case had on those who might speak out against the government, Dalkıran told her: "From the day we were arrested and the smear campaign by government media started, it was a clear message to the whole of civil society – and especially human rights defenders in Turkey – saying 'Stop!'"

She continued, addressing how government surveillance of online activity can make ordinary citizens targets: "It's not just human rights defenders [it's] basically anybody in Turkey right now. Before it was, OK, you tweeted against something so you are investigated; now if you like tweets you are at risk."

Another video in the series is an interview conducted by Mark Frary, associate editor for Index, with Maria Ordzhonikidze, director of Justice for Journalists Foundation.

JFJ has partnered with Index on a project to map attacks on media freedom under cover of the Covid-19 pandemic.

Ordzhonikidze explained how the governments in Russia and countries in the former Soviet Union have taken different approaches to curbing press freedom on the pandemic, from the denial of any coronavirus cases and the criminalisation of people who deviate from this line, to warnings and short-term detentions for journalists judged to have "spread panic" with their reports.

Russia, Kazakhstan, Azerbaijan and Uzbekistan take what Ordzhonikidze calls a "hybrid approach".

BELOW: JFJ director Maria Ordzhonikidze interviewed by associate editor Mark Frary for Index Shots. JFJ have partnered with Index for a mapping media freedom project

From the day we were arrested and the smear campaign by government media started, it was a clear message to the whole of civil society – Stop!

"In these countries the journalists, the independent journalists, and [the] media workers are punished and arrested for spreading fake news, for violating quarantine rules," she said. "They are forced to delete publications and they are beaten up."

On fake news laws, Ordzhonikidze echoed Dalkıran in saying that the oppression of free speech is not limited to traditional journalism.

"Anyone can be fined – not only the publication can be fined but any person, any blogger, any person who just retweeted the information or commented on the information."

Asked if this level of curbs on press freedom would be the new normal, Ordzhonikidze said: "Yes, I believe so. In countries like Russia definitely, there is no instrument to curb the authorities ... I don't see any indication of how this situation can be improved. I think it will only be worsened."

Index has recently appointed a new CEO, Ruth Smeeth (see more on page 50). Smeeth is a former MP for Stoke on Trent, England.

On joining Index, Smeeth said: "I'm excited to be joining Index on Censorship at a time when the organisation's work to protect free speech is more important than ever."

Index has also recruited a new youth advisory board which will sit until December. The board comprises eight people aged between 16 and 25 from around the world.

It includes Siphesihle Fali, an English and media student at the University of Cape Town, in South Africa; and Subhan Hasanli, a human rights lawyer in Azerbaijan, among others from countries including India, Spain and the USA. →

ABOVE: Index has just appointed a new youth advisory board for July to December 2020

LEFT: Index's first online magazine launch on Zoom was a discussion of privacy concerns in a new era of heightened surveillance. From left going clockwise: Spanish journalist Silvia Nortes; Index editor-in-chief Rachael Jolley; Turkish author Kaya Genç; African journalist Issa Sikiti da Silva; Ruth Smeeth, Index CEO

You have your choice to make. You take it easy or become a government enemy. Some people are giving up on journalism because of that kind of behaviour

→ A returning member of the board is AK Orr, a student from the UK. Speaking to Index about what they gained from sitting on the board in the previous term, Orr said: "Part of me had always imagined activism as being a solitary pursuit, but the youth board showed me that activism is inherently communal."

Orr added that it was vital for young people to engage in discussion about freedom of expression, saying: "We have to learn how to listen, fully listen, not just hear enough so that we retort to an argument we don't agree with."

In the midst of social distancing rules, Index held its first online magazine launch for the summer issue, where panellists discussed how surveillance could be used to curb freedom of expression.

"Here, in this kind of Zoom event, you never know. Maybe your event is

screened in the headquarters of the government, maybe 10,000 people are watching and you don't know, so that's a bit unnerving." said Kaya Genç, contributing editor at Index and a panellist at the event.

Joining Genç were Spanish journalist Silvia Nortes and Issa Sikiti da Silva, a journalist based in the Democratic Republic of Congo, who reports from across Africa. The panel was chaired by Index's Rachael Jolley.

Nortes commented on how older generations in Spain took a sceptical, critical view. "They are blaming the government for hiding information, for not being transparent with death data," she said. "As a consequence, they do not want to be controlled by a government that is lying."

Addressing the reality that in some African countries journalists cannot openly criticise those in power, Sikiti da Silva said: "You have your choice to make. You take it easy or become a government enemy. Some people are giving up on journalism because of that kind of behaviour."

Genç discussed how state surveillance and punishment could cause people to self-censor. "I think that's the biggest danger here – if we become self-surveillers."

Leah Cross, senior events and partnership manager at Index, emphasised the importance of the launch and similar online gatherings.

"These events are needed now more than ever," she said. "As we see governments using the pandemic to further stifle free speech, it's crucial that Index continues to provide a free, open and secure platform for discussion and debate." ⊗

BELOW: Özlem Dalkıran interviewed by Index editor-in-chief Rachael Jolley for Index Shots. Dalkıran is one of the Istanbul 10 who was accused of supporting a terrorist organisation

Orna Herr is the Tim Hetherington/Liverpool John Moores University fellow at Index

END NOTE

Spraying discontent

Where other types of protests are being closed down, street art is springing up, writes
Jemimah Steinfeld

49(03): 101/104 I DOI: 10.1177/0306422020958293

NIGHT-TIME, MOSCOW. THE streets would otherwise be quiet: the city is in lockdown and people are banished to their homes. But a group of activists are at work spray-painting walls and buildings around the city. Their slogans are simple, and convey opposition to Vladimir Putin's efforts to change Russia's constitution. These activists would ordinarily hold up placards and shout their discontent. But Putin's government has banned protests, even single person protests, under the guise of stopping the spread of Covid-19. Now their only option to have their voices heard is to scribble them on the country's public walls.

"Graffiti is one of the most free and independent ways to express yourself," said Russian artist RINO.Ink, who wrote "Content <<Freedom of Choice>> is not available in your region" in response to Putin's move. RINO.Ink knew it was illegal but believed "it is necessary to do this in order to cover this topic as much as possible".

"I find art the best way to say important and risky things and not be put in prison. I try to stay within the borders of law and use gentle hints, allusions and Aesopian language," added professional street artist Philippenzo Madonnaro, who lives in Moscow. Madonnaro tells Index that a week before the vote for the new constitution, he painted an artwork "Twenty" with Roman numerals to symbolise 20 years of Putin.

For Madonnaro, 20 years is too many years for someone to be ruling. He also added that he chose to mark this moment with the letters for 20 because "after 20 we get 21. And 21 is actually a blackjack, in Russian we call it "*ochko*", that could also have the rude meaning of deep asshole".

Russia's activists are not the only ones increasingly turning to street art in order to voice discontent. If anything, Covid-19 has provided a perfect moment for it. With museums, galleries and other cultural spots closed, and with protests being banned – or less desirable, given social distancing – one of the few ways to challenge authority is through street art.

And in the virus they've found a topic ripe for vibrant and thought-provoking commentary. Banksy, perhaps the world's most famous street artist, sprayed London's underground system "If You Don't Mask, You Don't Get" featuring a rat holding disinfectant.

Some artists are concentrating on the positives of the crisis, such as the key workers putting their lives on the line, as seen in work by Amsterdam-based street artist FAKE, whose mural "Super Nurse!" features a nurse wearing a facemask emblazoned with the Superman logo. Others are more critical of politicians.

Dominican street artist Jesus Cruz Artiles, aka EME Freethinker, painted US President →

RIGHT: Brazilian street artist Aira Ocrespo has been using his art to challenge the country's leader Bolsonaro

→ Donald Trump and Chinese leader Xi Jinping kissing through masks, and just days earlier completed a mural of a woman saying, "I don't trust in Bill Gates [,] China or USA!!".

In Brazil, the artist Aira Ocrespo has depicted President Jair Bolsonaro on several occasions since the outbreak. Bolsonaro has discouraged social distancing and lockdown, and was quoted as saying: "So what? What do you want me to do?" when asked about Brazil's fast rise in Covid-19 cases. The text reads "Bolsonaro's mask against the coronavirus". In another work, a picture of Bolsonaro taking a selfie has "Face death" written above it. "Brazil heading for the world's first pandemic," the artist writes on an Instagram post of the work.

With the art being in a public space, its impact is felt not just by those who are doing the work but by those observing it. Journalist Issa Sikiti da Silva, who is based in Uganda and travels to neighbouring countries, says he has noticed lots of images and slogans recently and is "moved and impressed".

"In a continent plagued by poverty, dictatorship, corruption, neo-colonialism and all sorts of social ills, some people take to the streets to express their displeasure and frustration about these challenges," he told Index. "Street artists take on the landscape, highly visible areas and public spaces, including highway walls, to draw different characters and slogans to send their message to whoever it may concern.

"These messages are often provocative, shocking, powerful, educational, among others. In some instances, street artists get in trouble with the local authorities if their graffiti messages are deemed critical to the regime, which instruct security forces to take them down and detain the authors.

Its impact is felt not just by those who are doing the work but by those observing it

"Street art is a form of freedom of expression which is not tolerated in many African countries, where dictatorship reigns and all forms of political and social art are deemed offensive to the ruling party."

Wachata Crew is a team of urban street artists from Tanzania. One member said: "Street art plays a big role in Tanzania, especially in matters of delivering messages in a unique and colourful way… Much of the population finds it more entertaining and convincing than [TV and newspapers]."

Wachata Crew stick within the legal framework and try to avoid issues that might be contentious and get them in trouble. But that still leaves room to cover important issues, including a large mural promoting mask wearing when Covid-19 was first in Tanzania, which was well-received.

Street art, and graffiti, its more basic bedfellow, are nothing new. From the dawn of humanity there are examples of it: prehistoric cave paintings in Burgundy, France; references to Virgil on the streets in Pompeii; messages written on the walls of Germany's Reichstag in 1945 by triumphant Soviet troops; red Chinese characters appearing all over the country during the Cultural Revolution. People have long been determined to express their views on public property.

Its forms vary from entire walls taken over by murals, which might often be officially sanctioned and approved, to simple one-word messages painted surreptitiously in the night.

And its practitioners cut across socio-economic borders.

"The creative urge to leave one's mark in public space crosses the boundaries of class, gender, sexuality, ethnicity and religion," said street art expert Richard Clay in an interview with the BBC.

Today, social media is also proving very useful in this field. Peter Bengtsen, author of Street Art and the Environment, told Index: "In many cases, street art and graffiti are no longer experienced in person … but rather through images on social media. Arguably, then, while the initial expression in the street certainly has importance

ABOVE: A mural done by Russian artist Philippenzo Madonnaro ahead of Putin's proposed constitution change

(as it perhaps creates a sense of authenticity in whatever message is being conveyed), its distribution on social media is incredibly important, as it has the potential to reach a much larger audience than the original street work."

Whether separated by class or country, the current crop of artists have one thing in common – they are using their art to hold power to account.

"Street art is important for political and social expression. It is part of our urban environments. It is not going away. It is an additional channel for people and groups to express their opinions and beliefs," said Jeffrey Ian Ross, an academic at the University of Baltimore and editor of the Routledge Handbook of Graffiti and Street Art, in an interview with Index.

"It is one of several types of communication that, if disseminated widely, can have a subtle impact on shaping how people respond to the pandemic," he said, adding that he'd "noticed a considerable amount of not just street art but graffiti during the pandemic".

He said street art could call attention to issues, such as Covid-19 and the death of George Floyd, and it could also "be an additional vehicle of communication when other means are prevented and or frustrated".

The authorities, which can take issue with women on display, thought it was about devil worship, so it was removed

ABOVE: Laila Ajjawi's mural of a Palestinian whose death was likened to the death of George Floyd

Bengtsen sees its role as crucial, albeit somewhat complicated, when it comes to free speech.

"Both graffiti and street art are ways to directly put a message out there. Stencils and posters are common ways to spread political messages, perhaps especially in authoritarian states where free speech is often severely limited," he said.

"On the one hand, street art and graffiti can be cast as tools of rebellion, free debate and democracy. They are potential ways for everyone to raise their voice. On the other hand, however, street art and graffiti can also be seen as decidedly undemocratic – as expressions that individuals force upon others by circumventing public decision-making."

However, to say that all are succeeding in their endeavours would be a stretch. In Russia, several of the activists-turned-artists have been arrested. And in Jordan, the artist Laila

Ajjawi says financial woes related to Covid-19 have curtailed her creativity. In order to make a living, and to simply afford the materials that go into street art, Ajjawi is largely reliant on commissions, but these have dried up. She hasn't stopped entirely – she recently did a piece on the death of Eyad al-Hallaq, a Palestinian whose killing in Jerusalem in June drew comparisons to the death of George Floyd.

Even in calmer times, Ajjawi said she had to get permission from the Jordanian officials for every piece she did – and that that can be hard. In some instances her work is removed even when she has been given permission. In 2016, for example, she drew an old woman with a city between her hands. The authorities, which can take issue with women on display, thought it was about devil worship, so it was removed.

"It was so sad … That was one of the biggest downs in my graffiti life," she told Index.

Ajjawi hopes the condition will improve soon so that she can do more artwork.

"Graffiti gives you a lot of power and makes me feel like I am doing my duty for my community," she said.

And what would she paint now if Jordan were her canvas? "I would do something that motivates people. Because of the pandemic, people are feeling very demotivated. Some people don't have anything and are very depressed. I would love to do something that boosts them, makes them think about themselves and how strong they are." ⊗

Jemimah Steinfeld *is deputy editor at* Index